FEDERAL PROPERTY POLICY IN CANADIAN MUNICIPALITIES

FIELDS OF GOVERNANCE:
POLICY MAKING IN CANADIAN MUNICIPALITIES
Series editor: Robert Young

Policy making in the modern world has become a complex matter. Much policy is formed through negotiations between governments at several different levels, because each has particular resources that can be brought to bear on problems. At the same time, non-governmental organizations make demands about policy and can help in policy formation and implementation. In this context, works in this series explore how policy is made within municipalities through processes of intergovernmental relations and with the involvement of social forces of all kinds.

The Fields of Governance series arises from a large research project, funded mainly by the Social Sciences and Humanities Research Council of Canada, entitled Multilevel Governance and Public Policy in Canadian Municipalities. This project has involved more than eighty scholars and a large number of student assistants. At its core are studies of several policy fields, each of which was examined in a variety of municipalities. Our objectives are not only to account for the nature of the policies but also to assess their quality and to suggest improvements in policy and in the policy-making process.

The Fields of Governance series is designed for scholars, practitioners, and interested readers from many backgrounds and places.

Federal Property Policy in Canadian Municipalities

Edited by

MICHAEL C. IRCHA AND ROBERT YOUNG

McGill-Queen's University Press
Montreal & Kingston • London • Ithaca

ISBN 978-0-7735-4134-4 (cloth)
ISBN 978-0-7735-4135-1 (paper)
ISBN 978-0-7735-8868-4 (ePDF)
ISBN 978-0-7735-8869-1 (ePUB)

Legal deposit third quarter 2013
Bibliothèque nationale du Québec

Printed in Canada on acid-free paper that is 100% ancient forest free (100% post-consumer recycled), processed chlorine free

McGill-Queen's University Press acknowledges the support of the Canada Council for the Arts for our publishing program. We also acknowledge the financial support of the Government of Canada through the Canada Book Fund for our publishing activities.

Library and Archives Canada Cataloguing in Publication Data

Federal property policy in Canadian municipalities / edited by Michael C. Ircha and Robert Young.

(Fields of governance; 5)
Includes bibliographical references and index.
ISBN 978-0-7735-4134-4 (bound). – ISBN 978-0-7735-4135-1 (pbk.)
ISBN 978-0-7735-8868-4 (ePDF). – ISBN 978-0-7735-8869-1 (ePUB).

1. Government property – Canada – Management. 2. Federal-city relations – Canada. 3. Municipal government – Canada. I. Ircha, M. C., 1945– II. Young, Robert, 1950– III. Series: Fields of governance; 5

JS1716.A9F43 2013   352.50971   C2013-901772-0

Typeset by Jay Tee Graphics Ltd. in 10.5/13 Sabon

Contents

Foreword

This is a collection of papers about federal property in Canadian municipalities, and the issues that property management and changes in ownership raise for communities. Public property is a very understudied field of public policy, especially as it concerns the various levels of government, and municipal government in particular. Policy about property owned by the federal government has changed a great deal over the past two decades. Notably, federal departments and agencies have been divesting themselves of surplus facilities of all kinds – ports, airports, military bases, and other installations – and these developments have had major ramifications for municipal governments across the country. It is worth studying the patterns of intergovernmental relations that these changes have engendered, and also the involvement of organized interests, especially business, in the politics of property decisions. This is the research presented in these chapters.

This collection of studies stands alone as a contribution to our knowledge about property issues in Canada. It is also, however, part of a larger project, one which has involved many scholars. The project concerns multilevel governance and public policy in Canadian Municipalities. It has many components, but the biggest part of the work has been done on policy fields in various provinces and in municipalities of different sizes, as in the studies collected here. The objective of the work, very briefly, is to document what policies exist in a variety of fields and to explain their character; that is, to show how the policies came about, first as a function of the processes of intergovernmental negotiation through which they were shaped, and second as a function of the pressures and demands of various social forces, or organized interests, that were involved in the policy process. More information about the project is available at http://www.ppm-ppm.ca.

Some acknowledgments are in order. First we wish to thank the Social Sciences and Humanities Research Council of Canada for its support through the Major Collaborative Research Initiatives program. The University of Western Ontario and other universities contributed generously to the project. We thank McGill-Queen's University Press for its continued interest in our research. Nicole Wellsbury helped prepare the final formatted manuscript of this work with care and professionalism. We thank Jen Lajoie for compiling the index. Finally, we acknowledge the contribution of Kelly McCarthy, who served as project manager for the whole research enterprise. She coordinated various research meetings and conferences and handled the flows of manuscripts, and we are grateful for her work.

Michael C. Ircha and Robert Young

FEDERAL PROPERTY POLICY IN
CANADIAN MUNICIPALITIES

I

Introduction

MICHAEL C. IRCHA AND ROBERT YOUNG

Federal and provincial governments often occupy significant parcels of land within Canadian municipalities. From a local government perspective, land and property ownership by other levels of government can be both beneficial and detrimental to the host municipality. Unlike the federal and provincial governments, whose jurisdictions are defined in the Constitution Act, 1982, municipalities find themselves subservient as a statutory government operating under provincial authority. The ownership and use of federal property have often created a difficult relationship with the local host municipality. The use of public lands by the federal government often brings public servants, with steady and well-paid jobs. Federal facilities create spin-off jobs, contributing to the local economy as clients of local businesses. The services offered by the federal government can raise the municipality's regional, national, and even international profile – adding to the community's attractiveness for economic development. On the other hand, a municipality's inferior status as a statutory government renders it relatively powerless in dealing with "senior" governments, which lie beyond the legal jurisdiction of the municipality and thus may ignore local by-laws and other municipal legislation and regulations.

For example, the absence of municipal authority was evident in the early development of telecommunication towers for wireless cellular phones, when Communications Canada ignored planning rules and other local by-laws in issuing permits for their construction. Telecommunications were considered to be in the national interest and thus superseded local land use planning rules. After municipal concerns were raised across the country, steps were taken by the federal government to consult with local authorities to seek the appropriate accommodation of these new technological devices (Townsend 2004), but this was in no way mandatory.

Another more perennial example is the case of payment of property taxes to the local municipality. In the past, federal government departments and agencies provided a "grant-in-lieu" of taxes to municipalities. But such grants were often considerably less than the amount that the municipality would have received from private sector taxpayers occupying the same property. More recently, the federal government modified its position and now provides "payments in lieu of taxes" (PILTs) that more closely conform to the property tax payments that would have arisen through municipal assessments. However, there are still limits on the payments being made by some federal agencies. They argue that they should pay not the full assessment, but only the portion they deem to reflect the specific services received from the municipality. A 2012 Supreme Court decision has reinforced the federal minister's discretionary authority in setting PILTs in a fair and equitable manner, but not necessarily at the same level as the local municipal assessment (*Halifax (Regional Municipality) v. Canada (Public Works and Government Services)*).

This collection of case studies focuses on the policy issues arising from the presence of federal lands and properties within municipal jurisdictions. Our objective is to identify potential means of improving federal-municipal land use, management, and transfer, by considering intergovernmental relationships and the involvement of the community. This book principally considers the federal-municipal relationship with respect to federal properties in the light of several case studies involving federal land transfers, both successes and failures. It also deals with issues surrounding occupancy and use.

We are interested in several theoretical questions about how policies about federal lands are made, through intergovernmental relations and under the pressure (or not) of various social forces. The questions are laid out below. Our methodology is fairly straightforward. We selected four provinces that differ in size, political culture, and federal presence, and that may fairly represent Canada's diversity. In three of the provinces – New Brunswick, Newfoundland and Labrador, and British Columbia – research teams explored federal property issues in several municipalities. These were selected because federal property is important in each of them. We did not study more provinces because of resource constraints, yet we could not study fewer because we expected that municipal-federal relations would be mediated in various ways by provincial governments (Garcea and Pontikes 2006) and we needed interprovincial variation to understand these differences. We also chose municipalities of various sizes, again to seek representativeness so that we could investigate relations in different types of municipalities. We particularly sought to include smaller places that are often neglected in municipal research. In all, we have case studies concerning twelve municipalities in these provinces, which is unprecedented in this policy field.

In Ontario, the approach was different. Only one case study was selected – the Toronto waterfront. This is a very important case for the province and for Canada as a whole. It may represent major initiatives such as Halifax's harbour, the Port of Montreal, and the development of Granville Island and False Creek in Vancouver. In any event, we have one very complex case studied in great detail, over a long period of time. This adds considerable depth to the collective research, and it can help test the generalizations that we derive from the material as a whole.

The researchers employed a range of methods. The case studies rely on thorough analysis of government documents of many kinds – studies, annual reports, expenditure data, press releases, and so on. For relatively contemporary events that are mainly of local interest, newspaper accounts are invaluable. The Toronto waterfront study alone involved sifting through over 2,000 newspaper items. Where possible, secondary sources were used, but it should be stressed that property is a policy field that has attracted very little scholarly analysis in the disciplines of political science and public administration. (One purpose of our research is to help fill this gap and to attract more attention to the field.) Finally, the researchers all engaged in interviews with politicians and officials from all three levels of government and from various social actors involved in property issues. A total of thirty-eight interviews were undertaken in the course of the research reported here.

Federal property issues can be approached from several perspectives: centre versus periphery, constitutional versus statutory government, and industrial versus post-industrial aspects. Considerable concern can be raised about large-city biases in dealing with federal-municipal issues. The majority of Canadians live and work in large urban areas; however, as is evident in the case studies, it is enlightening to consider as well the difficulties facing smaller municipalities in their relationships with the federal government, especially when they are located far from central Canada and on the periphery of the nation. As well, municipalities suffer from being statutory governments (that is, established under the authority of a provincial statute) rather than being constitutionally based (Tindal and Tindal 2004). Finally, societal change from the former industrial phase, with its focus on manufacturing, to the current post-industrial era has instituted a sea of change in municipal land use. Former industrial lands, now known as "brownfield" sites, are being transformed for new residential, recreational, and commercial uses. Federal properties are being caught up in the changing currents of a consumer-oriented society. Federal lands are being declared surplus as departments and agencies consolidate their holdings in an era of downsizing and rationalization. The societal shift to post-industrialism is also reflected in the rise of the "creative class" of knowledge workers (Florida 2002). Consumer demand for municipal and other government services is changing, and this has direct implications for the current and future uses of urban land.

The next section of this Introduction considers the relevant federal legislation that helps to shape the federal-municipal relationship with respect to federal lands. The following section provides a national overview of federal-municipal land concerns. Then we lay out the theoretical issues and questions that guided the research. This is followed by a brief summary of each chapter.

RELEVANT FEDERAL PROPERTY LEGISLATION

At the beginning of the 1980s, the industrialized world entered an era of neo-liberalism exemplified by "Thatcherism" in Britain and "Reaganism" in the United States. This shift to the right was partly driven by the severe financial crisis faced by many governments following rapid inflation and subsequent recession in the early 1980s. Dramatic and radical cuts to various public sector operations were made throughout the world, unleashing a drive towards New Public Management (NPM), with its focus on making government more efficient by employing private sector approaches and establishing market conditions for the delivery of public services (Savoie 2003, 337). NPM focused on the privatization of assets, the contracting-out of service delivery, performance appraisal, and policy evaluation

(Osborne and Gabler 1993). The goal of NPM was "to break down formal systems of control and instill a new 'bias for action' in government bureaucracies" (Savoie 2003, 12–13). New Public Management signalled a radical change from government's former focus on inputs and processes to a new emphasis on performance and results within a more transparent accountability framework (Aucoin 1996).

Canada did not escape this swing to the right of the political spectrum and the introduction of New Public Management. With the election of Brian Mulroney's Progressive Conservative government in 1984, Canadians witnessed a new era of program evaluation and deregulation. In effect, the Mulroney government sought improved efficiencies by adopting NPM concepts aimed at making the public sector function more like the private sector. Soon after the election an "ad hoc" Ministerial Task Force on Program Review was put in place, chaired by the deputy prime minister, Erik Nielsen. The Nielsen Task Force, aided by its twelve-member private sector advisory panel, reviewed some 989 federal programs representing expenditures totaling $92 billion (Saint-Martin 2000). Although many senior public servants opposed what they saw as the "slash and burn" mentality of the Task Force, the government did succeed in ushering the concepts of New Public Management into the federal public service. One outcome of the Nielsen Task Force was the subsequent privatization of several major Crown corporations such as Air Canada and, later, the Canadian National Railway. Another outcome was to make the first systematic and comprehensive inventory of federal property (Canada, Task Force on Program Review 1986). A third result was the passage of the Federal Real Property Act of 1992, which aimed to simplify and modernize the government's property management practices, and to adopt the practices of conveyance commonly found in the private sector (Treasury Board 2009).

Less than a decade after the Nielsen Task Force, facing substantial budget deficits and rapidly growing public debt, Jean Chrétien's 1993 Liberal government took major steps to reduce federal expenditures. Part of this involved divesting itself from direct government involvement in many sectors. For example, Transport Canada entered into a major divestiture program to shed its ongoing operational responsibilities for facilities such as national airports and many smaller ports and harbours.[1]

Surplus federal lands and properties, such as large former military bases, were to be divested by the Canada Lands Company (CLC), a federal commercial Crown corporation established in 1995. The CLC's primary goal is "to ensure the commercially oriented, orderly disposition of surplus properties with optimal value to the Canadian taxpayer" (Canada Lands Company 2012). Operating at arm's length from the federal government and – notably – without government funding, the CLC purchases strategic federal surplus land and properties at market value from various departments, agencies, and Crown corporations in order to revitalize the lands and reintegrate them into their local communities. The CLC's value-added function enhances the value of federal surplus lands by developing the sites and selling properties to generate the maximum financial return to Canadian taxpayers. The Canada Lands Company's mandate and actions exemplify some of the core principles of New Public Management with its clear economic focus on the disposal of federal lands and property.

A growing number of critics suggest that New Public Management has peaked and the concept is in decline. They argue that the core business and private sector values inherent within New Public Management run counter to the values found in traditional democracy. For example, Terry (1998) argued that public entrepreneurs (such as the CLC model) tend to be oblivious to such democratic values as fairness, justice, representativeness, and participation. As pointed out by Kernaghan and Siegel (1987), the fundamental administrative values in the Canadian public service that run counter to New Public Management include neutrality, accountability, efficiency and effectiveness, responsiveness, and representativeness. Mingus (2007) raised the question of whether or not New Public Management introduced different values into the public sector, leading to private interests superseding public interests.

FEDERAL PROPERTY – A NATIONAL PERSPECTIVE

There are many issues and challenges that emerge in dealing with federal lands within municipalities. In the chapter on British Columbia, Somerville, Wilson, and Young introduce a distinction between "perennial" issues and "dynamic" issues. Perennial issues involve continuing matters, such as the level of PILTs contributed by the federal government to municipal coffers in lieu of property taxes, the upkeep of properties, and conformity with municipal plans and standards. Dynamic issues involve particular federal initiatives about their property. In some cases, the federal government is seeking to acquire property. In recent years, for example, in the process of decentralizing federal services from Ottawa to other parts of Canada, the National Research Council (NRC) sought property in various university-related communities to establish new research laboratories and offices. However, more common in recent years are instances of property divestment. As a result of program reductions and rationalization, federal departments and agencies have sought to divest themselves of surplus lands and property. In the transportation sector, for example, divestment has led to the devolution to local agencies of airports and ports. The most significant and at times most controversial transfer of federal lands has come from the disposal of surplus military bases. The Canada Lands Company has been a key player in disposing of surplus federal lands.

Canada's Ports and Urban Waterfront Development

Pressure to convert commercial waterfront land to alternative uses is a continuing source of conflict between ports and their municipal hosts. A survey of Canada's seventeen major commercial ports designated as Canada Port Authorities (CPA) under the Canada Marine Act of 1998 found that seventy percent of them experience such conversion pressure (Ircha 2002).[2] The most common alternative use sought for the port's commercial lands is to provide public access to the waterfront, followed by demands for residential use (highrise apartments and townhouses), parks, recreational walking trails, and waterfront roads. As one port manager put it, "The most significant pressure is from adjacent municipalities and their Official Community Plans. These exercises tend to be driven by public opinion; hence parks and access to the waterfront become high priority, high profile issues" (Ircha 2002, 9). But port managers are also cognizant of their customers' needs and of the broader regional and national economies. Another manager explained, "[There is] a complete lack of understanding by the communities that their port serves the interests of six million Canadians, not just them, and their actions/requests can have a severe detrimental effect on families and communities 2–3,000 kilometers away" (Ircha 2002, 9).

These comments echo an earlier study of Canadian ports that found urban planners and municipal councils were more interested in waterfront rejuvenation to support city centre revitalization than were the port managers, as the latter tended to focus on waterfront redevelopment for marine cargo handling and shipping services (Hoyle 1992).

The concept of waterfront revitalization and redevelopment began in North America: "in the 1960s and 1970s, the United States and Canada were the cradles of the waterfront-redevelopment movement" (Hoyle 1988, xviii). The most emulated project was Boston's Faneuil Hall and Quincy Market. This project created the prototype of a "festival marketplace" as a recreation-oriented locale to attract people. Similar waterfront projects can be found in Canadian ports, including the Historic Properties in Halifax, Market Square in Saint John, *Le Vieux Port* in Montreal, Toronto's Harbourfront, and Granville Island in Vancouver.

The intimate linkage between a city and its port is a historic reality. But during the past century, this linkage has increasingly been attenuated by technical and economic change. Larger ships and their increased cargo capacity forced ports to seek more space for docking and landside cargo storage. As city-centre land costs soared and availability declined, ports were forced to seek downstream alternatives. A good example of this trend is Vancouver's development of additional container handling facilities at Deltaport, located at Roberts Bank in the Strait of Georgia. In turn, as inner-city port lands became less important for marine cargo handling, opportunities often arose for the conversion of these properties to other urban-oriented uses.

One of the major trends impacting existing port facilities is the public's strongly rising demand for access to and use of waterfront lands. In ports around the world, politicians, municipal officials, NGOs, and citizens' groups are exerting pressure to convert port lands to alternative uses. Today's affluent urbanites seek the development of waterfront condominiums, walking trails, parks, cafés, and boutique shopping areas in place of under-used, unsightly industrial port lands.

As development proceeds, the proponents and subsequent tenants of urban-oriented waterfront residential and commercial development enjoy the presence of the port's busy terminals and active harbour area. But they soon tire of the cargo-handling noise (particularly in the evening and night time hours), dust, noxious emissions from equipment and ships, light spillage from the terminal, congestion from truck and rail traffic, and other detrimental aspects of marine cargo-handling operations. As a result, nearby residents mount pressure to constrain the port's commercial terminals by seeking municipal regulations to limit the terminals' hours of operation, reorient dockside lighting, and restrict truck traffic on city streets. In the extreme, commercial marine terminals have been forced to shut down and move their operations to more remote locations. For example, over the years in Sydney, Australia, many port operations have been curtailed and relocated to nearby Botany Bay (Ircha 2000). This shift in the location of commercial cargo handling led to Sydney Harbour becoming known worldwide as an attractive tourist and recreational facility, but such development came at a high cost to the original marine terminal operators. This same trend of waterfront land conversion to urban-oriented uses is occurring in many of the world's major ports (Gordon 1997).

Waterfront land is a non-renewable resource, so conflict is almost unavoidable. Most port lands in Canada are owned by the federal government, and are managed by Canada Port Authorities (CPAs). The Canada Marine Act of 1998 created CPAs as independent Crown agencies. Like Canada's airport authorities, CPAs are non-shareholding, non-profit corporations operating under Letters Patent issued by the federal government. The authorities manage federal port lands and assets, are expected to be financially self-sufficient, and contribute an annual stipend based on the port's gross revenues to the federal government.

While the host municipality and its citizens often seek access to the waterfront for urban-oriented redevelopment, CPAs try to retain their waterfront lands for possible future cargo-handling opportunities. In some cases, such resistance to converting waterfront lands has been beneficial to both the port and the municipality. For example, the growth of cruise ship traffic in many Canadian ports has benefitted municipalities' tourism activities. These large passenger ships typically seek berths close to city centres for the convenience of their tourist passengers. In many Canadian ports, there has been considerable capital investment in cruise terminal facilities and associated amenities, allowing cruise passengers to disembark close to the city centre. This is a beneficial situation for the host municipality as well. In Saint John, for example, the Port Authority is an active partner in the Waterfront Development Plan, and its new cruise ship terminal complements the city's investment in improving Water Street. Cruise ship passengers enjoy aesthetic and convenient access to the shops and activities in the nearby city centre, and local businesses benefit from the visiting shipborne tourists. The growth in cruise ship traffic complements Saint John's substantial waterfront development, Market Square, which transformed a former general cargo wharf into a retail and community facility on the central waterfront through federal, provincial, municipal, and private investments (Schuyler and Ircha 1987).

Urban planners generally seek the so-called "highest and best use" for land development. The best use is generally a fair and equitable combination of economic return from the land's development with social, cultural, and other community values that reflect the broader public interest. The issue is how to determine the public's interest in waterfront land use. In the community versus ports debate, there must be a clear understanding by decision-makers at all levels of government of the difference between local and regional (and national) interests. There are also short-term and long-term implications of the decisions being made. Converted waterfront land cannot easily be reconverted to commercial cargo-handling activities. Thus shifting waterfront lands to urban-oriented uses means the long-term loss of this land for port purposes.

The resolution of conflicting values reflected in waterfront land issues is a complex process. An essential requirement is a dialogue leading to a better understanding of the goals and objectives of both municipalities and ports. Today, most firms and public agencies speak of the need to obtain a "social license" to operate from their host communities. As Pierre Lassonde (2003, 9) described it, "social license is the acceptance and belief by society, and specifically local communities, in the value creation of your activities." Improving relations with host municipalities requires ports to be more transparent and accountable. The port's social license must first be earned by creating credibility and trust and then continually maintained (Ircha 2012). Dealing effectively with port-community relations requires continued dialogue based on trust. As pointed out in the *Eldman Trust Barometer* (2010, 6), prepared for the World Economic Summit in Davos, Switzerland: "For the first time, this year's Trust Barometer shows that trust and transparency are as important to corporate reputation as the quality of products and services. In the u.s. and in much of Western Europe, these two attributes rank higher than product quality – and far outrank financial returns." Trust is essential in dealing with issues between ports and their host community. A social license is based on the beliefs, perceptions, and opinions of the local community; it is granted by the community (in other words, a network of stakeholders); and it is intangible, dynamic, and non-permanent – a social license is subject to change as new information is acquired. A social license to operate is a form of constructive engagement in which the port and its stakeholders work together to achieve mutual goals.

Airport Divestiture

Throughout much of the twentieth century, airports in Canada evolved as a federal responsibility. Following World War II, all major public airports were planned, built, and owned by the federal government (Dion 2002). From the 1960s through to the 1980s, airport development and operations were the responsibility of the Canadian Air Transportation Administration (CATA), as a part of Transport Canada. The Treasury Board provided capital funding for infrastructure investments in runways, terminals, and other buildings. Revenues generated through landing fees, terminal charges, and ticket taxes were consolidated in a Revolving Fund. This Fund was used to support airport operations across the system. As pointed out by Dion (2002, 1), "It was, in effect, a means for cross-subsidization whereby surplus revenues generated at the large busy airports could be transferred to smaller airports with inadequate revenues." Under CATA jurisdiction, individual airports were not required to be self-financing or to have break-even operations. Airport managers had little incentive to increase their revenues or improve their cost-efficiency (Padova 2007). Further, airport development decisions were made centrally at a national level with little regard for the community significance of airports at regional and local levels.

The Canadian air transportation system experienced considerable growth in the 1970s coupled with rapid improvements in aircraft technology. New technology led to increased flying ranges that eliminated the need for intermediate airports (such as at Gander in Newfoundland, formerly used as a refuelling stop for trans-Atlantic flights). Growing passenger volumes led the federal government to build Mirabel Airport, a considerable distance from Montreal's Dorval (now Trudeau) Airport, and to acquire lands in the Pickering area for a proposed major airport to supplement Toronto's Malton (now Pearson) Airport. A 1979 report of Transport Canada's Task Force on Airport Management recommended establishing autonomous airport commissions for Canada's major airports (Transport Canada 1979). This recommendation mirrored the contemporary creation of relatively independent Local Port Corporations under the Canada Ports Corporation. However, little action was taken on the Task Force recommendations (Dion 2002).

By the 1980s, the federal government had become concerned about the growing scope of Canada's airport system and its increasing cost (Raynor 1994). These concerns were reflected in several ways. A study team report on Real Property for the 1985 Nielsen Task Force on Program Review recommended that "the government should also consider instituting a fundamental change in policy for airport operations from ownership and centralized public service operations to locally managed and owned airports" (Canada 1986, 28–9). The May 1985 federal budget indicated that "the government will pursue the development of a new management structure for the federal airport system in Canada." In October 1985, the minister of Transport appointed an Airports Task Force. In its 1986 report, the Airports Task Force recommended transferring airports to local authorities, with Transport Canada retaining responsibility for safety and security (Dion 2002).

Based on the Airports Task Force's recommendation, in 1987 the minister announced a new airports policy reflecting the view that local management of airports would be more efficient and responsive to community concerns. In essence, the policy indicated that the government was prepared to entertain proposals for transferring ownership and/or operations from provinces, municipalities, local authorities, or the private sector (Dion 2002). Although no legislation was adopted to provide the basis for this ministerial statement, Transport Canada officials undertook negotiations to transfer five of Canada's major airports. In 1992, four private, not-for-profit local airport authorities (LAAs) were established in Vancouver, Calgary, Edmonton, and Montreal (the last including both Dorval and Mirabel Airports). The transfer agreements were lengthy and complex legal documents whereby these major airports were leased for sixty years under a defined rental payment formula. Through this arrangement the federal government retained ownership of the airports. Negotiations to transfer the Toronto airport were concluded in 1993; however, the proposed lease to the private sector became a federal election issue and was subsequently cancelled by Jean Chrétien's new Liberal government.

In 1993, Alti Rodal and Nick Mulder published a seminal paper outlining a typology of power-sharing relationships involved in transferring federal properties. They concluded that a not-for-profit partnership with government would be more accountable to citizens than transferring federal properties either to the private sector or to another level of government (Rodal and Mulder 2003). As Mulder was the deputy minister of Transport during the subsequent period of airport transfers, it was not surprising that there was no apparent interest in privatizing airports (Brooks and Prentice 2001).

The Liberal government adopted a formal National Airports Policy in 1994. By this time the full extent of Canada's fiscal problems and deficit situation had became public knowledge. It was generally concluded that the federal government's intention was to devolve airports as a means of downloading their growing cost. However, securing enhanced competitiveness as a reflection of New Public Management was also a factor. As pointed out by the minister of Transport, Doug Young, "what this nation must have is an integrated and affordable national transportation system. One that emphasizes safety and reliability. One that is efficient. And one that builds strong, viable companies in all modes" (Transport Canada 1994a, 1).

There were concerns about the earlier LAA lease agreements. They did not include public accountability principles, membership on LAA Boards of Directors was not defined by the federal government, and rent payments to the federal government proved to be burdensome, while the LAAs' ability to maximize their resources was constrained (Brooks and Prentice 2001). The 1994 National Airport Policy (NAP) set out to rectify some of these concerns in a new approach:

> Canada requires a national airport system comprised of airports that are safe, commercially oriented and cost effective … [T]hose who benefit most directly from the services or facilities provided must pay a fair share of the costs … The federal government will retain ownership of the 26 airports identified as part of the National Airports System. However, under the NAP they will be leased to Canadian airport authorities. These local operators will be responsible for financial and operational management. (Transport Canada 1994b, 2)

The National Airport Policy's goal was to enable community-based not-for-profit airport authorities to "develop their airports, reduce costs, tailor levels of service to local demand, and attract new and different types of business. This policy encouraged airport authorities to be financially self-sufficient and gave them freedom to determine how to fund their operations" (Transport Canada 2007, 1).[3]

The NAP defined the twenty-six airports within the National Airports System (NAS) as those handling more than 200,000 passengers per year as well as those located in national, provincial, or territorial capitals. These NAS airports handled ninety-four percent of all of Canada's air passengers and cargo. Leases with the airport authorities were to be for sixty years with a twenty-year renewal option. Membership on locally constituted boards of directors would include representatives from chambers of commerce; boards of trade; consumer, labour, and professional groups; and federal, provincial, and municipal governments. Canada's other numerous regional and small airports were to be transferred to local interests with a new Airport Capital Assistance Program to provide financial support for safety-related capital projects. The assistance program was important in generating local commitment to acquire smaller airports, which was not the case for small ports (Dion, Slack, and Comtois 2002). Arctic airports were offered to territorial governments under the Arctic Airports Transfer Program (Transport Canada 1994b).

Negotiating transfer agreements with Canada Airport Authorities (CAA) was complex and difficult, often taking several years. The auditor general subsequently reprimanded Transport Canada for its approach to these negotiations, citing a failure to determine each airport's fair market value and a lack of a framework for determining the financial impact of the transfer process (Auditor General 2000).

Concerns about the initial LAA approach were addressed in the new policy through the requirements of a public accountability framework built into CAA lease agreements. Community representation was provided for in the CAA Board composition. The lease required each CAA to hold an annual stakeholders' meeting, provide public advertising of impending fee changes, tender major contracts, and create a community consultation committee.

Despite such arrangements, the new CAAs and the existing LAAs continued to generate controversy. The airline industry soon realized that there was no mechanism for them to resolve disputes with the airport authorities (Tretheway 2008). CAAs could exercise their monopoly powers to establish new fees and charges provided that they were duly advertised. The airlines were concerned that new expenses would raise the costs of flying and deter future passenger growth (hence the current trend of listing all fees and charges on airline tickets to ensure passengers realize the extent of external costs to the airlines).

The airlines' fears were soon realized, as many of the medium and smaller NAS airports understood that with the lack of cross-subsidization from major airports, their long-term financial viability was questionable. This economic concern led to the establishment of Airport Improvement Fees and then Passenger Facilitation Fees. Ostensibly, these charges were to be used to support the airports' capital development. However, a portion of revenues was soon directed to support airport operations. The auditor general found that these fees were an increasing source of revenue for airports and that Transport Canada had been slow in assessing their reasonableness (Auditor General 2000).

The financial challenge facing medium and small CAAs is their inability to generate sufficient reserve funds to offset future capital investment requirements (Tretheway 2008; Seaman 2009). Transport Canada's growing security and safety regulations and requirements have driven up CAA costs and reduced the ability of smaller CAA airports to generate the required capital reserves. Essentially, many small airports serve as feeders to the major hub airports. During the previous regime, Transport Canada would have ensured cross-subsidization across the airport network, but this has ceased under the NAS. Feeder airports tend to be financially hard-pressed, while hub airports generate significant surplus revenues and build major new terminals to accommodate their growing business (Ircha 2001).

In March 2003, Bill C-27, An Act Respecting Airports, Airport Authorities and Other Airport Operators, was introduced in the House of Commons. This legislation was drafted by Transport Canada following its five-year NAS review and in response to the auditor general's criticisms. Bill C-20 subsequently died on the Order Paper following second reading (Padova 2007). New legislation was introduced in the House of Commons in June 2006 as Bill C-20, the Canada Airports Act. The bill consisted of 253 sections clarifying the minister's roles and responsibilities and focusing on detailed and prescriptive approaches to governance, board responsibilities and duties, establishing and revising fees, preparing land use plans, and reporting on environmental incidents (Tretheway 2008; Padova 2007). The CAAs and the Canadian Airports Council (CAC) criticized several aspects of Bill C-20, in particular constraints on the airports' ability to operate in a commercial manner. The CAC's concerns included proposed restrictions on revenues that could interfere with necessary capital improvements, the appeal mechanism for airport fees and charges, and the impact of enhanced directors' liability (Canadian Airports Council 2006). However, like its predecessor, Bill C-27 failed to proceed beyond second reading.

Canada's National Airports System is composed of twenty-six not-for-profit airport authorities. Although concerns persist about appeal mechanisms for fees and charges, the sustaining of uneconomical medium and small NAS airports, and how the national interest is being met by this set of separate independent entities, there have been beneficial results from Canada's airport devolution process. The auditor general (2000, 10–16) pointed out: "Transport Canada notes that a number of aspects of the transfer initiative have been positive and that airport authorities have made some strategic choices that have also represented difficult operational decisions. These included, for example, the expansion of passenger facilities, liberalization of operating policies and relocation of scheduled traffic from one airport to another." Tretheway (2008, 150) indicated that Vancouver's new international terminal was not in Transport Canada's capital plans: "there is no question that needed capital investment in the terminal would not have been made without the transfer of the facility to the airport authority." Montreal modified its two-airport structure by shifting most air traffic to Dorval and leaving Mirabel to serve air cargo. This critical decision meant the Montreal CAA had to make considerable capital investments at Dorval (Trudeau) Airport. Both Calgary and Edmonton made investments to increase their terminal capacity, which had not been planned earlier by Transport Canada. In Toronto, the new CAA purchased the privately owned third terminal. It then built a new terminal to address growing capacity problems at the airport. Similarly, in Ottawa, Winnipeg, and Halifax, new terminals were developed; these had not been anticipated by Transport Canada.

In summary, a key federal policy goal in the airport devolution process has been achieved. There has been considerable increased investment in Canadian airports without the need for additional tax-based funding. Capital enhancements at many CAA airports have enabled the national airports system to generally accommodate increased passenger volumes. But several challenges remain. Appropriate future policies and programs are required to address the need for an appeal mechanism for fees and charges and for future capital investments at medium-sized and smaller NAS airports.

The Canada Lands Company and Surplus Military Bases

The Canada Lands Company (CLC) was established in 1995 as a self-financing federal commercial Crown corporation, during the federal government's era of deficit reduction, cost recovery, and partial implementation of New Public Management. The CLC seeks to optimize the financial and community value of strategic government surplus properties through effective planning, including rezoning and site servicing for property development, so as to achieve the highest and best use of the land. The CLC receives no government appropriations and contributes its profits to the federal government. Since its formation in 1995, the CLC has provided over $373 million to the Government of Canada (Canada Lands Company 2010, 2).

The CLC has had both successes and failures in dealing with federal land transfers. Recently, the CLC was awarded a LEED ND (Leadership in Energy and Environmental Design for Neighbourhood Development) gold certificate for a section of its Village at Greisbach in Edmonton, which represented the successful transformation of a former military base to a "new urbanism" style of sustainable residential development (Village 2009).[4]

The CLC generally seeks to increase land use density, following new urbanism approaches to develop livable communities on surplus federal lands. But the CLC's mandate is to maximize the financial return from land development – it "undertakes projects that provide financial returns to the Government of Canada" (Canada Lands Company 2008, 1). In cases where other aspects of public interest may be sought (such as the Downsview case, discussed below), the CLC has created subsidiary corporations reporting directly to Parliament. The CLC currently has two subsidiary corporations: Parc Downsview Park Inc. and Old Port of Montreal Corporation Inc.

Until November 2006, the Federal Treasury Board classified surplus federal property as either routine or strategic. These were defined as follows:

Routine disposal: Surplus real properties subject to routine disposal are generally properties or a portfolio of properties with lesser value that can be sold easily without any substantial investment. These properties are normally sold in their "as is" state on the open market by the custodian, its agent (Public Works and Government Services Canada), or a private sector firm. "As is" transactions imply that there is limited potential for increasing the value of the property prior to sale or transfer and that there are no strategic interests in the property.

Strategic disposal: Surplus real properties subject to strategic disposal are properties or portfolios of properties with potential for significantly enhanced value, those that are highly sensitive, or a combination of these factors. Because of the complexity associated with these properties, they may require innovative efforts and a comprehensive management approach to move them into the market. Canada Lands Company CLC Limited, as the government's disposal agent, disposes of these selected surplus properties through a strategic disposal process. (Treasury Board 2001, 1)

Despite the CLC's claim to respect community values, there has been ample evidence to the contrary, in the cases covered in this collection and elsewhere. This is the nub of the conflict between the perspectives and objectives of the federal and municipal governments in the federal property realm. The CLC's handling of strategic surplus federal lands is aimed at maximizing the government's financial return, while the municipality's goal is generally to gain an asset for public use.

The more recent Treasury Board "Directive on the Sale or Transfer of Surplus Real Property" seeks to address some of this conflict with communities over federal transfers. It provides for "a whole of government perspective; efficiency, equity and transparency in transactions; best value to the Canadian taxpayer; *consideration of the interests of communities and other levels of government*; and the *fulfilment of any legal obligations with respect to Aboriginal groups*" (Treasury Board 2006, 2, emphasis added).

Several of the case studies outlined in the following chapters deal with the closure and subsequent transfer of surplus military bases. These include facilities at Argentia and Happy Valley–Goose Bay in Newfoundland and Labrador, Chatham in New Brunswick, and

Chilliwack in British Columbia. Other bases and lands surplus to the needs of the Canadian Forces have also been defined by the Treasury Board as strategic and sold to the Canada Lands Company for eventual transformation to alternative uses. To complete a national perspective on the divestiture of military bases, we should briefly consider issues related to Downsview in Toronto and the Kapyong Barracks in Winnipeg. For an excellent analysis of the closing of CFB Summerside, see Savoie (1995).

The former Downsview air force base in the north end of Toronto was closed in the early 1990s. The then minister of National Defence, David Collenette, proposed to the federal cabinet that the 231-hectare site be redeveloped as a park. As discussed by Horak (2012), the federal government indicated in 1995 that the site should be self–financing, with half the land being used as a park and the other half redeveloped for commercial and residential purposes to fund the park project. However, the Department of National Defence (DND) was reluctant to transfer the land at less than market value. In 1997, the Canada Lands Company (CLC) was directed by the federal government to create a subsidiary corporation to develop the Downsview lands.

Parc Downsview Park Inc. (PDP) began operations in 1999 with a separate board of directors appointed by and reporting to the minister of Infrastructure. But PDP had difficulties: the DND still owned the land, and the CLC's mandate is selling federal lands at market value, not redeveloping them for public use on a cost-recovery basis. This conflict between obtaining an optimal financial return on the lands and providing for their public use as a park continued for several years. In 2006, the land title was finally transferred from the DND to PDP for a nominal sum.

But by this time, community expectations had been raised by earlier public pronouncements by the federal government, not least during a site visit by Prime Minister Chrétien and Minister David Collenette, in which they unveiled plans for a $40 million park to be constructed within months (Kuitenbrouwer 2003). There was a general misconception that the whole site was to be a park. So when PDP unveiled a draft plan with large-scale residential and commercial development on the lands, there was local consternation (Downsview Lands Community Voice Association 2007). In addition, the City of Toronto was resentful that PDP was using its federal status to plan the site's development, bypassing the municipality's planning process.

In 2007, the federal government addressed apparent multilevel governance conflicts by replacing PDP's board of directors. The new board sought to improve relations with the City of Toronto by agreeing to abide by the municipal planning process, despite the delays to construction that this step would engender. Site construction began in 2009, completing the lengthy fifteen-year process for transferring and developing this important parcel of federal land (Parc Downsview Park 2009).

Another long and controversial military land transfer process involves the Kapyong Barracks in Winnipeg. This 91-hectare site consists of two distinct parcels: 52 barracks and warehouses, and 358 military-built homes (National Defence 2007). Kapyong Barracks was the former location of the 2nd Battalion, Princess Patricia's Canadian Light Infantry (2PPCLI), prior to its redeployment to CFB Shilo in western Manitoba. The lands sit between two of Winnipeg's wealthiest neighbourhoods, River Heights and Tuxedo; hence the Kapyong site is a prime location for redevelopment. Although 2PPCLI moved out in 2004, the base was actually declared surplus in 2001 (Robbins 2009). In the normal course of events, a strategic land parcel of this nature would be transferred to the Canada Lands Company for redevelopment and sale. In January 2003, the CLC established a Winnipeg office and appointed a project manager for the Kapyong site to develop plans and liaise with relevant municipal officials (Leo and Pyl 2007). The CLC planned to develop the Kapyong Barracks as a mixed-use sustainable and compact residential neighbourhood in the New Urbanism style. The City of Winnipeg supported these plans and looked forward to obtaining added right-of-way on its arterial road, Kensington Avenue, which bisects the Kapyong site (Welch 2009a).

In November 2007, the Treasury Board ordered the sale of the military lands to the CLC. But in January 2008, the seven Treaty One First Nations filed a court injunction to stop the sale (Rabson and Welch 2009). By the fall of 2009, the lands had not been transferred to the CLC, its Winnipeg office had closed, and there was no reference to the Kapyong Barracks on the CLC website (Welch 2009b).

There were two main issues that opposing groups focused on. First, most of the 358 military houses on the site were sitting empty, while Winnipeg's need for well-maintained affordable housing continued to rise. The city requested some of the housing, but federal officials in Winnipeg could not obtain the authority needed to respond favourably (Leo and Pyl 2007). The second and likely more crucial issue was the possibility of converting the Kapyong Barracks to an urban reserve for the Peguis and Brokenhead First Nations. A claim under Treaty Land Entitlement (TLE) was made for the lands before the 2PPCLI vacated them. TLE is a collection of agreements that give First Nations the right, and the money, to acquire surplus federal lands, in situations where they have not received their proper allocation of reserve lands according to treaties signed between 1870 and 1910 (O'Brien 2003; Treaty Land Entitlement Committee 2009). The First Nations were seeking the Kapyong Barracks site as an urban reserve for schools, housing, and businesses to create jobs for their people (Welch 2009c). This First Nations claim effectively stalled the land transfer and subsequent development of the Kapyong Barracks site.

In 2009, the First Nations claim for the site was considered by the Federal Court, with the federal government arguing the First Nations had no right to the surplus lands as it had already paid the bands money in lieu of land, thus nullifying their treaty land entitlements. The First Nations argued they had not been consulted on the availability of the surplus federal lands at Kapyong Barracks. Justice Douglas Campbell upheld the First Nations' arguments by ruling that they still had an entitlement and should be consulted before any land was transferred or any development occurred on the site (Rabson 2009). The federal government appealed the judge's ruling (Cohen 2009).[5] In 2011 the Federal Court of Appeal found that the lower court had not assessed the facts of the case properly and ordered another Federal Court hearing on the issue. The retrial is scheduled for December 2012 (Rabson 2012).

This case, as will be elaborated in the British Columbia chapter, shows how First Nations have emerged as a key player in intergovernmental relations, as opposed to being seen as another normal non-governmental organization reflecting a specific aspect of societal interest. Such considerations lead directly to the theoretical questions that have guided our research.

THEORETICAL ISSUES

The issues about federal property that are described and analyzed here have arisen within a particular historical context. Many factors have contributed to changes in municipal-federal relations and to new patterns of public policy. Globalization, for one, has affected societies and governments in profound ways. Increased global flows of trade, investment, people, and information all influence policy-making in Canadian municipalities, as elsewhere (Sassen 2000). Increased pressures for international competitiveness have raised concerns about government deficits, leading to services being cut and downloaded to other levels of government. These pressures are strikingly evident in the field of federal property. But more generally, policy issues in municipalities have become increasingly salient to more people, a phenomenon sometimes called "glocalization" (Courchene 1995). Large cities are seen by some as the engines of economic growth, essential for competitiveness (Savitch and Kantor 1995), but new economic pressures challenge all municipalities, even the smallest. Another factor is demographic change. Urbanization continues to increase, and in Canada it is supplemented by large flows of new immigrants. Major cities must accommodate new residents. Yet the demographic challenge in much of Canada, especially in smaller towns in peripheral regions, is how to cope with a declining population and a shrinking industrial and resource base. These background problems are evident in several cases examined here.

Another development is that values and attitudes have changed. Canadians, like the citizens of most advanced industrial countries, now show less deference to established elites and elected politicians; they are less inclined to be passive consumers of policy (Nevitte 1996). Instead, citizens are concerned with democratic participation, which is most feasible at the municipal level. Technological change is a final background factor. This poses new problems and opportunities in every policy field, but it also affects political participation because of the dramatic decline in communications costs. The internet, e-mail, and social media have made it easy for individuals to make new connections. They facilitate the organization in particular locales of like-minded people around issues of all kinds (Stanbury and Vertinsky 1995). They also open up wider strategic opportunities, for vertical linkages can be forged more easily with groups organized at the regional, provincial, and national levels, and demands can be registered directly with policy-makers at these different scales.

These factors constitute the backdrop to issues about federal property, and define the general theoretical setting of our research. The work presented here, though, focuses on those who directly engage in shaping public policies; that is, upon governmental actors and social forces. By "social forces," we refer to more or less formally organized interests, including trade unions, business associations, cultural and other groups, and civil-society organizations of all kinds. These agents are the proximate causes of policy. We have particular theoretical interest in two areas – how intergovernmental relations affect policy and how social forces are engaged in the policy process.

We expect that intergovernmental relations will help shape policies about federal property in municipalities. To explore this requires, first, a study of the linkages between municipal governments and the federal government. Although this relationship has long been neglected, there are signs that Ottawa has developed a renewed interest in municipalities (Young and Leuprecht 2006), though this has moderated under the Conservative government led by Stephen Harper. Intergovernmental negotiations are obviously crucial in many property issues, and so we want to track how these levels of government interact in this policy field. Second, we cannot neglect the provincial governments, which oversee municipalities. The provinces generally mediate municipal relations with the federal government, but their stance in this regard varies widely across provinces and policy fields (Garcea and Pontikes 2006). We want to explore this variation and its effects on policies about property. Third, we are interested in the role of politicians in this field. The normal interactions between levels of government involve officials, who often can work smoothly together because of long association and shared expertise. But politicians establish the parameters within which officials work, they become involved in decision-making when problems arise, and they can champion issues and causes. So what is the role of politicians in making policy about federal property, and what effect do they have on the character of policy? Do ideological differences between politicians come into play in this policy field?

Intergovernmental relations are conducted by actors with goals and resources. The distribution of resources among actors is critical in shaping the resulting policy. We are interested in the resources at the disposal of municipal, federal, and provincial actors; in particular, we want to understand how the relative balance of resources affects the character of public policy. Next, we are concerned with New Public Management (NPM). The widespread adoption of its principles has led to changes in most public bureaucracies. Many functions have been delegated to specialized agencies, commissions, and public-private partnerships, while administrative hierarchies have been flattened and officials' range of discretion increased. We have already observed that NPM underlies important changes in Ottawa's overall policies about its property, such as the CLC's mandate and values. How did the principles and practices of NPM affect the nature of outcomes about particular property issues?

Our second concern about federal property policy is the interplay of governments and social forces. The collaboration of citizens, more or less organized, with state actors is central to the modern notion of "governance" (Rhodes 1996). There are several reasons why such collaboration has increased over the years – the resource constraints faced by governments, rising citizen demand for participation, and the need for information for policy-making, for example. Here, we are not interested in such causes, but rather in how social forces interact with policy-makers and in what influence they have on policy.

First we need to know what groups are involved in the field. Then our interest turns to the stages of the policy process – agenda-setting, proposing policy alternatives, decision-making, and implementation (Pal 2006). We want to assess when different social forces are involved, because earlier participation in policy-making normally means greater influence on the policy. So how does the pattern of involvement affect the character of policy about federal property?

A particular concern here is with business. There is a very large body of literature about the connection of business interests with the local state. Some theorists argue for a "growth machine" model where municipalities compete to serve business interests (Peterson 1981); others suggest that coalitions between business and other social forces can produce redistributive policies (Stone 1989); still others hold that policy fields are fragmented and no one interest dominates all fields (Dowding 2001). We need evidence about whether business is paramount in policy-making at the local level and in intergovernmental arenas. We also want to know whether other social forces engage in policy conflicts with business interests and whether they can win policy concessions. These are important questions to ask about federal property issues.

There is also the question of the strategies employed by social forces. Intergovernmental policy-making involves three levels of government and extensive horizontal networks of social actors. So we are interested in whether social forces attempt to create broad coalitions in order to increase their influence on public policy. A related question concerns the scale at which local social forces are capable of operating. Intergovernmental decision-making involves distant actors at the provincial and national levels. Are social forces able to transcend the municipal level? Do they have the capacity to engage actors in higher levels of government, either directly or through allies?

All of these issues constitute the theoretical preoccupations that guided the research in the chapters presented in this collection. We will return to them in the Conclusion. There, we also take up our final question: how good are the policies about federal property? We do aim to assess the quality of policy, using various criteria. Can we identify good policies and procedures? Further, we ask whether there are changes in the process of policy-making, especially in the conduct of intergovernmental relations and the participation of social forces, that would produce better policies.

THE CONTRIBUTIONS

The following three chapters provide provincial perspectives on specific cases of federal-municipal land issues. The fourth chapter focuses on federal land concerns relating to the Toronto waterfront development process.

To begin, Tracy Summerville, Gary Wilson, and John Young introduce the distinction between perennial issues and dynamic issues relating to federal property. This is a valuable contribution. Perennial issues are those that reflect the day-to-day administration of federal properties and their relationship with the interests of municipal governments. Dynamic concerns, on the other hand, are more controversial and arise from federal government initiatives. These provoke policy responses and negotiations that generally involve all three levels of government: municipal, provincial, and federal. They also stimulate much citizen attention and efforts by various social forces to shape policy outcomes. Summerville, Wilson, and Young demonstrate the application of perennial and dynamic approaches in their evaluation of the new container terminal in Prince Rupert and Prince George's airport redevelopment to attract international passengers and cargo. Both of these projects are components of the federal government's Asia-Pacific Gateway and Corridor Initiative. Further exploration of perennial and dynamic approaches is reflected in the authors' consideration of the transformation of CFB Chilliwack to civilian uses, and the revitalization of Vancouver's downtown harbour area. Summerville, Wilson, and Young also consider the issue of First Nations' claims on federal lands and the implications of these claims for subsequent development. This is a vital issue in British Columbia and many other parts of Canada, even where treaties have long existed.

Kurt Peacock and Robert MacKinnon explore several federal land projects in New Brunswick. The study of the closure of CFB Chatham and its transformation into Sky Park Miramichi shows that success still eludes this site. On the other hand, the conversion of the former Canadian National Railway Maintenance Shops in Moncton to alternative community uses has surpassed expectations, reflecting a different socio-economic context and a strong combined political effort at the municipal and provincial level. Peacock and MacKinnon's consideration of Saint John's inner harbour provides a rich case study of this federal port and its municipal relations. The community desire for alternative waterfront development conflicted with the Saint John Port Authority's need to maintain its commercial marine activities. Over time, compromises and adjustments on both sides led the Port Authority to become an active partner in the Saint John Waterfront Development Corporation, which aimed to improve community access and use of inner harbour waterfront lands. The Fredericton cases involve both federal land acquisition and airport devolution. The federal government's National Research Council initiated a search for a location for its new IIT e-Business Centre in New Brunswick. Their request for bids led to a competition among educational institutions in partnership with their municipal hosts. Fredericton and the University of New Brunswick's acquisition of this major NRC research laboratory offers a successful case of federal land acquisition. Another case – the transfer of Transport Canada's Fredericton Airport to an airport authority – outlines the many challenges municipalities face in negotiating with federal officials. In both of these instances, success was dependent on strong municipal and provincial political support.

Stephen Tomblin, Wade Locke, and Jeff Braun-Jackson provide a compelling review of difficult municipal-federal relations in Newfoundland. They argue that Newfoundland's history of having strong political leaders and its sense of isolation from the rest of Canada have led to a focus on self-reliance and territorial self-determination.

Federal-municipal relationships are further complicated by Newfoundland's strong urban-rural divide. Small communities outside of St John's are suspicious of top-down, urban-biased proposals for transformative change. As a result, there are considerable difficulties in launching new ideas, building coalition support, and gaining public trust. The authors demonstrate the relative powerlessness of smaller, peripheral municipalities in dealing with their federal counterparts on federal land issues. The lack of capacity and resources at the local level and the absence of strong provincial political support have led to inadequate responses to federal land transfer arrangements. Effectively, without provincial intervention, there is a highly unequal power relationship between federal and municipal officials dealing with land matters.

Tomblin, Locke, and Braun-Jackson explore these difficulties in the cases of Placentia, Argentia, and Happy Valley–Goose Bay. Their findings reveal a lack of federal accountability and transparency in dealing with their municipal counterparts. The lack of guidelines in Ottawa to deal with unique properties leaves municipal officials frustrated and sensing themselves powerless to influence decision-making in faraway centres. Further, the lack of financial and staff resources at the municipal level limits communities' ability to effectively lobby for their interests in Ottawa and other decision-making centres.

Christopher Sanderson and Pierre Filion provide an extensive history of the complex and controversial issues concerning federal lands in the Toronto waterfront development process. Their analysis demonstrates the pitfalls of intermittent federal attention to waterfront issues, and of the creation of unique agencies to deal with contemporary concerns. As each agency was established with a specific goal, conflicts arose over time as circumstances changed while mandates did not, and complexity made conflict resolution difficult. Sanderson and Filion point out that one of the agencies, the Canada Lands Company, has a mission to maximize revenues from surplus federal land sales, rather than to optimize community values. Thus, the goals and priorities of the various agencies often conflicted with the waterfront planning objectives of municipal, metropolitan, and provincial governments.

The authors deal with controversial Toronto Port Authority issues such as the Toronto Island Airport. The continued operation of the airport and the proposed bridge crossing over the West End Channel led to bitter disputes between city hall and the Port Authority.

They also study the expansive industrial area in the east harbour area, known as the port lands, which was wrested away from the Port Authority and conveyed to the Toronto Economic Development Corporation, an independent arm of the City of Toronto. Subsequent litigation and ongoing disputes laid the groundwork for continuing conflict in port-municipal relations on Toronto's waterfront. This chapter offers a rich study of a myriad of multilevel governance issues in a complex and highly visible case.

The Conclusion sums up the results of the studies. It draws out general comparative findings. As well, it uses comparisons to address the theoretical issues guiding the research. Interestingly, we find that many standard issues about multilevel governance have a poor fit with the dynamics of federal property issues. This field broadens our understanding of policy-making because it involves a prominent and measurable characteristic – the value of land and other property. Finally, we attempt to assess the quality of policies about federal property and we then make suggestions to improve outcomes in this field. These practical matters are important in all policy research.

So let us proceed to our case studies of federal property and multilevel governance.

NOTES

1 For a comparison of the divestiture of ports and airports in Quebec, see Dion, Slack, and Comtois (2002). Municipalities found ports a much less attractive proposition than divested airports.

2 Note that the issues identified here do not apply only to the larger ports. See Debrie, Gouvernal, and Slack (2007).

3 For an account of the various models of airport ownership and management structure that have appeared worldwide, see Gillen (2011). Canada is unique in adopting a model of independent, not-for-profit corporations.

4 The principles of new urbanism have been outlined in the Charter of New Urbanism as: "[N]eighborhoods should be diverse in use and population; communities should be designed for the pedestrian and transit as well as the car; cities and towns should be shaped by physically defined and universally accessible public spaces and community institutions; urban places should be framed by architecture and landscape design that celebrate local history, climate, ecology, and building practice" (Charter 2009).

5   The current CLC policy holds that "[i]n making decisions on the disposal
    of Crown properties that could affect aboriginal groups' rights, title, or
    treaty rights, the Government of Canada must respect the fiduciary rela-
    tionship between the Crown and aboriginal groups, as confirmed by the
    Supreme Court of Canada, and fulfill any federal fiduciary obligations as
    they relate to the interests of aboriginal groups."
       But note: "This is the responsibility of the Government of Canada, and
    not CLC." In other words, other departments handle fiduciary matters
    before the CLC takes possession of the lands (Canada Lands Company
    n.d.).

REFERENCES

Aucoin, P. 1995. *The New Public Management: Canada in Comparative
    Perspective*. Montreal: Institute for Research on Public Policy.

Auditor General of Canada. 2000. "Transport Canada – Airport Transfers:
    National Airports System." Chapter 10, *2000 October Report of the
    Auditor General of Canada*. Ottawa.

Brooks, M., and B. Prentice. 2001. "Airport Devolution: The Canadian
    Experience." Discussion Paper, Centre for International Trade and
    Transportation. Halifax: Dalhousie University.

Canada Lands Company. 2008. "2008 Annual Public Information Ses-
    sion." http://www.clc.ca/learn-more-about-clc/mandate-values.

– 2010. *Reaching Out Annual Report 2009–2010*. n.p. Canada Lands
    Company Limited.

– 2012. "Canada Lands Company Limited: Homepage." http://www.clcl.
    ca.

– n.d. "Policy Respecting Corporate Relations With Aboriginal Groups."
    http://www.clc.ca/policy/policy-respecting-corporate-relations-
    aboriginal-groups.

Canada, Task Force on Program Review. 1986. *Real Property: A Study
    Team Report to the Task Force on Program Review*. Ottawa: Minister
    of Supply and Services Canada.

Canadian Airports Council. 2006. "Bill C-20: CAC Six Issues Supplement."
    Briefing Document. Ottawa: Canadian Airports Council.

"Charter of the New Urbanism." 2009. http://www.cnu.org/charter.

Cohen, E. 2009. "Government Appeals Court Ruling on Kapyong." *Win-
    nipeg Free Press*, 31 October.

Courchene, T.J. 1995. "Glocalization: The Regional/International Inter-
    face." *Canadian Journal of Regional Science* 18, no. 1: 1–20.

Debrie, Jean, Elisabeth Gouvernal, and Brian Slack. 2007. "Port Devolution Revisited: The Case of Regional Ports and the Role of Lower Tier Governments." *Journal of Transport Geography* 15: 455–64.

Dion, J.P. 2002. "Airports in Transition." PRB 02-41E. Ottawa: Science and Technology Division, Parliamentary Information and Research Service, Library of Canada.

Dion, S., Brian Slack, and Claude Comtois. 2002. "Port and Airport Divestiture in Canada: A Comparative Analysis." *Journal of Transport Geography* 10: 187–93.

Dowding, K. 2001. "Explaining Urban Regimes." *International Journal of Urban and Regional Research* 25, no. 1: 7–19.

Downsview Lands Community Voice Association. 2007. "Newsletter." Vol. 1, no. 1.

Eldman Trust Barometer. 2010. Davos, Switzerland: World Economic Summit.

Florida, Richard. 2002. *The Rise of the Creative Class.* New York: Basic Books.

Garcea, Joseph, and Ken Pontikes. 2006. "Federal-Municipal-Provincial Relations in Saskatchewan: Provincial Roles, Approaches, and Mechanisms." In *Canada: The State of the Federation 2004 – Municipal-Federal-Provincial Relations in Canada,* 333–67. Montreal & Kingston: McGill-Queen's University Press for the Institute of Intergovernmental Relations.

Gillen, David. 2011. "The Evolution of Airport Ownership and Governance." *Journal of Air Transport Management* 17: 3–13.

Gordon, D. 1997. "Managing the Changing Political Environment in Urban Waterfront Development." *Urban Studies* 34, no. 1: 61–83.

Halifax (Regional Municipality) v. Canada (Public Works and Government Services), 2012 SCC 29, Docket 33876.

Horak, M. 2012. "Multilevel Governance in Toronto: Overcoming Coordination Challenges in the 'Megacity.'" In *Sites of Governance: Multilevel Governance and Policy Making in Canada's Big Cities,* edited by Robert Young and Martin Horak, 228–62. Montreal & Kingston: McGill-Queen's University Press.

Hoyle, B.S. 1988. "Introduction." In *Revitalizing the Waterfront,* edited by Hoyle et al., xviii. London: Bellhaven Press.

– 1992. "Waterfront Development in Canadian Ports: Some Viewpoints on the Issues Involved." *Maritime Policy and Management* 19, no. 4: 279–95.

Interviews A and B, 2001. Confidential survey of CPA CEOs on waterfront redevelopment pressures being exerted.

Ircha, M.C. 2000. "Global Port Reform: An Australian Focus." In *Proceedings* of the Annual Conference of the Association of Canadian Port Authorities. Charlottetown PEI.

– 2001. "Presentation on Airports." Research Seminar, National Transportation Act Review Commission. Montreal.

– 2002. "Port Privatisation: Commerce and Recreation." In *Proceedings* of the Annual Conference of the International Association of Maritime Economists. Panama City, Panama.

– 2012. "Social License for Ports." *Canadian Sailings: Transportation and Trade Logistics*, 12 March: 17–22.

Kernaghan, K., and D. Siegel. 1987. *Public Administration in Canada: A Text*. Toronto: Methuen.

Kuitenbrouwer, P. 2003. "Chrétien Gives Blessing to Downsview Park Remodeling." *National Post*, 30 September.

Lassonde, P. 2003. "How to Earn Your Social License." *Mining Review*, British Columbia and Yukon Chamber of Mines, Vancouver, Summer: 7–13.

Leo, C., and M. Pyl. 2007. "Multi-Level Governance: Getting the Job Done and Respecting Community Difference – Three Winnipeg Cases." *Canadian Political Science Review* 15, no. 2: 1–25.

Mingus, M. 2007. "Investigating Ownership Values as a Catalyst of Financial Scandal in Canada's Public Sector." *The SAIS Review of International Affairs*, XXVII, no. 2: 1–23.

National Defence. 2007. "The Strategic Disposal of CFB Winnipeg (South); Kapyong Barracks and the South Side Housing Lands." http://www.admpa.forces.gc.ca/news-nouvelles/news-nouvelles-eng. asp?cat=03&id=2531.

Nevitte, N. 1996. *The Decline of Deference: Canadian Value Change in Cross-National Perspective*. Peterborough ON: Broadview Press.

O'Brien, D. 2003. "Brokenhead First Nation Stakes Claim on Kapyong." *Winnipeg Free Press*, 16 December.

Osborne, David, and Ted Gabler. 1993. *Reinventing Government: How the Entrepreneurial Spirit is Transforming the Public Sector*. New York: Penguin.

Padova, A. 2007. "Airport Governance Reform in Canada and Abroad." PRB 07-12E. Ottawa: Economics Division, Parliamentary Information and Research Service, Library of Canada.

Pal, L.A. 2006. *Beyond Policy Analysis: Public Issues Management in Turbulent Times*. 3rd ed. Toronto: Thomas Nelson Publishing.

Parc Downsview Park. 2009. "Downsview Park; A Glimpse into the Future." http://www.downsviewpark.ca/eng/illustrations.shtml.

Peterson, P.E. 1981. *City Limits*. Chicago: University of Chicago Press.

Rabson, M. 2009. "Kapyong Land Transfer Invalid: Federal Judge." *Winnipeg Free Press*, 30 September.

Rabson, M. 2012. "Half of Kapyong on Offer: Source Says First Nations Mulling Ottawa's Deal." *Winnipeg Free Press*, 29 November.

Rabson, M., and M.A. Welch. 2009. "Judge Freezes Kapyong." *Winnipeg Free Press*, 1 October.

Raynor, R.N. 1994. "Potential for Privatization: Halifax International Airport." *Proceedings*, Canadian Transportation Research Forum: 965–78.

Rhodes, R.A.W. 1996. "The New Governance: Governing without Government." *Political Studies* 44: 652–7.

Robbins, H. 2009. "Peguis, Brokenhead Win First Round of Kapyong Battle." *The Interlake Spectator*, 12 November.

Rodal, A., and N. Mulder. 1993. "Partnerships, Devolution and Power-Sharing: Issues and Implications for Management." *Journal of Public Sector Management* 24, no. 3: 27–48.

Saint-Martin, D. 2000. *Building the New Managerialist State: Consultants and the Politics of Public Sector Reform in a Comparative Perspective*. Oxford UK: Oxford University Press.

Sassen, S. 2000. *Cities in a World Economy*. 2nd ed. London: Pine Forge Press.

Savitch, H.V., and P. Kantor. 1995. "City Business: An International Perspective on Marketplace Politics." *International Journal of Urban and Regional Research* 19, no. 4: 495–512.

Savoie, Donald J. 1995. "Summerside: Revisiting the Base Closures." *Canadian Journal of Regional Science* 18: 57–76.

– 2003. *Breaking the Bargain: Public Servants, Ministers and Parliament*. Toronto: University of Toronto Press.

Schuyler, G., and M.C. Ircha. 1987. "Market Square: Downtown Economic Revival." *Plan Canada* 27, no. 1: 16–22.

Seaman, R. 2009. "An Airport Is Worth How Much? Underestimating Its Economic Benefit to the Community." *Wings*, May–June.

Stanbury, W.T., and I.B. Vertinsky. 1995. "Assessing the Impact of New Information Technologies on Interest Group Behaviour and Policy-making." In *Technology, Information and Public Policy: Proceedings of*

a Conference Held at Queen's University 17–18 November 1994, edited
by T.J. Courchene, 293–379. Kingston: John Deutsch Institute for the
Study of Economic Policy.

Stone, C.N. 1989. *Regime Politics: Governing Atlanta, 1946–1988.*
Lawrence KS: University Press of Kansas.

Terry, L.D. 1998. "Administrative Leadership, Neo-Managerialism, and
the Public Management Movement." *Public Administration Review* 58,
no. 3: 194–200.

Tindal, Richard C., and Susan Nobes Tindal. 2004. *Local Government in
Canada.* 6th ed. Toronto: Nelson.

Townsend, David A. 2004. *Report on the National Antenna Tower Policy
Review.* Ottawa: Industry Canada.

Transport Canada. 1979. *Task Force on Airport Management: Progress
Report.* Ottawa: Canadian Air Transportation Administration.

– 1994a. Transport Minister Douglas Young Speech, National Transportation Day.

– 1994b. *National Airports Policy.* Ottawa: Transport Canada.

– 2007. "National Airports Policy." http://www.tc.gc.ca/eng/mediaroom/
backgrounders-b04-a008e-2238.htm.

Treasury Board. 2001. "Treasury Board Policy on the Disposal of Surplus Real Property." http://www.tbs-sct.gc.ca/pubs_pol/dcgpubs/Real-
Property/dsrp-abie-PR-eng.asp?printable=True.

– 2006. "Directive on the Sale or Transfer of Surplus Real Property."
www.tbs-sct.gc.ca/pol/doc-eng.aspx?id=12043§ion=HTML.

– 2009. "Guide to the Federal Real Property Act and Federal Real Property Regulation." http://www.tbs-sct.gc.ca/pubs_pol/dcgpubs/tb_g3/reg-
1-eng.asp.

Treaty Land Entitlement Committee. 2009. "The Manitoba Treaty Land
Entitlement Framework Agreement." http://www.tlec.ca.

Tretheway, M.W., and R. Andriulaitis. 2008. "Airport Policy in Canada:
Limitations of the Not-for-Profit Governance Model." In *Aviation
Infrastructure Performance: A Study in Comparative Political Econ-
omy,* edited by C. Winston and Gines de Rus, 136–44. Washington DC:
Brookings Institute.

"Village at Griesbach Receives LEED ND Certification." 2009. Green Business: Strategies for Corporate Sustainable Development. 10 September.

Welch, M.A. 2009a. "Kensington Plan Leaves Unanswered Questions."
Winnipeg Free Press, 14 September.

– 2009b. "Kapyong Battle Drags On." *Winnipeg Free Press,* 11 September.

– 2009c. "Judge Delays Kapyong Review." *Winnipeg Free Press,* 21 May.

Young, R.A., and C. Leuprecht, eds. 2006. *Canada: The State of the Federation 2004 – Municipal-Federal-Provincial Relations in Canada*. Montreal & Kingston: McGill-Queen's University Press for the Institute of Intergovernmental Relations.

2

Federal Property in British Columbia: Dynamic Changes and Perennial Issues

TRACY SUMMERVILLE, GARY N. WILSON,
AND JOHN F. YOUNG[1]

The devolution and divestiture of federal property[2] in British Columbia have initiated dynamic changes and highlighted perennial issues in intergovernmental relations and in the interaction of social forces with government agencies. Dynamic changes are those that have created opportunities and incentives for property development and altered intergovernmental relations. In some cases, such developments were welcomed locally as an answer to economic woes, and new intergovernmental relationships were formed that were cooperative and positive. In other cases, however, development was viewed as an intrusion, and intergovernmental relations were strained as local government and social forces mobilized to criticize federal policies about property.

In the area of the perennial, day-to-day administration of federal properties, intergovernmental relations unfolded in a more traditional manner, as local governments dealt with the bureaucratic and fiscal changes that followed new legislation. Perennial federal property issues tended to involve few actors outside of government, and municipal governments were policy takers rather than policy-makers. Responses to such perennial issues often came from federal- and provincial-level municipal associations rather than from particular municipalities.

Perennial intergovernmental relations did not create groundswell responses from multiple actors. In contrast to the dynamic intergovernmental relations that arose from the devolution or divestiture of federal property, perennial intergovernmental responses occurred within a hierarchical relationship between federal and municipal governments. For example, perennial federal property issues, such as Payments in Lieu of Taxes (PILT), tended to follow federal decisions, with very little or no involvement from the provincial government or social forces.

Dynamic federal property issues, on the other hand, created very elaborate policy communities involving all three levels of government and a variety of social forces. Even in dynamic issues, however, the federal government tended to play the role of initiator, with other levels of government and social forces reacting to and having to deal with the impact of federal decisions.

In order to explore these issues in more depth, this chapter examines four communities in British Columbia: Prince Rupert, Prince George, Chilliwack, and Vancouver. The communities represent four distinct regions of the province of British Columbia. They also vary in size, and in their socio-economic makeup. These municipalities allow us to identify themes and patterns common throughout the province. All of these communities have federal properties for which they receive annual payments in lieu of taxes from the federal government, and which involve other perennial issues. More significantly, however, federal policy concerning the use or divestiture of federal property has brought change to all four communities. In each case, new policies regarding federal property introduced a significant number of new actors into the policy arena, which would not have happened if the federal government had not divested property or devolved power to local governments.

These four municipalities will be used to highlight some of the main issues in intergovernmental relations between federal, provincial, local, and First Nations' governments, and the involvement of social forces in the policy process and in debates concerning the management and development of federal property in British Columbia. In particular, this chapter explores some of the unique features of the policy context in British Columbia, as well as the actors and processes which are common in other parts of Canada.

The chapter begins with an overview of the political context and current policies that have shaped both the dynamic and perennial aspects of federal property regulation. Following a brief introduction to each of the communities, part two briefly sketches some perennial federal property issues. Part three explores the intergovernmental dynamics and social forces that influenced dynamic federal property issues in British Columbia. The last section suggests some recommendations about the existing policy process that would facilitate the management of federal property issues in the province.

POLITICAL CONTEXT AND CURRENT POLICIES

While British Columbia shares many concerns about federal property with other provinces, the province has a few unique and important contextual features that clearly differentiate it from the rest of Canada. First, and most important, Aboriginal land claims in British Columbia remain largely unresolved. In many parts of the province, land claims and treaty settlements are in the process of being negotiated, and vast areas of land, including lands held by the federal government, are considered by First Nations to be part of their traditional territories. The unpredictable nature of property relations in the province, especially in the area of dynamic federal property issues, differentiates British Columbia from many other jurisdictions in Canada.

Second, British Columbia is one of the only provinces with an independent property assessment authority. BC Assessment replaced municipal and provincial government assessment offices in 1974. This independent and publicly funded corporation was created by legislation to produce and maintain uniform property assessments across the province, based on market value, which is considered the fairest way to assess property (BC Assessment 2008). However, although BC Assessment assesses all property across the province, including federal property, it appears that the federal government does not take the assessments into account in its PILT to the municipalities. Instead, the federal government uses its own assessment of property values – an assessment that, according to most municipal officials, is almost always lower than the provincial assessment (Interview 5). This discrepancy is one of the issues that complicate federal-municipal relations over perennial federal property matters in British Columbia.

Third, the recent growth in trade with Asia over the last couple of decades has transformed British Columbia into a key part of the federal government's Asia-Pacific Gateway and Corridor Initiative (APGCI). Although somewhat slow to respond to this opportunity, successive federal governments have supported the development and expansion of coastal ports and transportation corridors as a means of building the APGCI. This policy has created a number of significant infrastructure projects in the province that have been both aided and hampered by changes in the administration of federal property.

Finally, in British Columbia and indeed throughout the West, it appears that there is still a sense, whether real or perceived, of geographical and political separation from Ottawa. In many respects, issues that have arisen in the area of federal property management have fed general perceptions of alienation, poor communication, and a lack of federal responsiveness to local needs. This is particularly true in the area of perennial federal property issues such as PILT, where municipal governments have little or no recourse when a lessee of federal property is in arrears on municipal taxes. While some may argue that the institutional deficiencies of federalism are the main cause of this disconnect, interviewees in our study were more inclined to blame geography. Such geographical and political separation is also evident in the more dynamic changes that have taken place in recent years. For example, in many cases of dynamic change, the province and municipalities often have to accept federal divestiture decisions with little or no input prior to the decision being made. The closing of the Canadian Forces Base in Chilliwack and the accusations of "partisan politics" underlying that decision were a case in point. Such perceptions fuel the fires of Western alienation and undermine trust in the federal government.

FEDERAL PROPERTY ISSUES IN FOUR COMMUNITIES: CHILLIWACK, VANCOUVER, PRINCE GEORGE, AND PRINCE RUPERT

In order to understand the intergovernmental relations and social forces that shape federal property issues in British Columbia, four cases were chosen that best represent the province as a whole. The selection of cases takes into account a number of important variables, including geographic location, city size, and the type of economy. As noted above, these four cases also involve the most dynamic federal property issues that have occurred in the province in recent years. The data on these cases was gleaned from interviews with municipal officials and non-governmental actors, including business interests. A significant portion of the study is also based on media reports and other secondary sources. These sources have proven particularly helpful in shedding light on the intergovernmental and community dynamics of federal property issues in each case.

Chilliwack (population 72,000) is located in the Fraser Valley, about 100 kilometers east of the City of Vancouver. Incorporated in 1873, the city is one of the oldest municipalities in British Columbia. Its main industries are food processing, agriculture, and forestry. For many years it was the home of Canadian Forces Base (CFB) Chilliwack. The base was officially closed in December 1997, and the property was divested in 2001 as part of the federal government's plans to consolidate military operations and initiate cost savings by selling surplus federal property. This decision was initially met with considerable opposition in Chilliwack, and in British Columbia more generally, because of the economic impact on the city and the fact that the closure would deprive the province of a land forces presence. Since the closure, however, the city and the province, along with other public and private actors, have taken advantage of this prime real estate by pursuing a number of different projects, including an education park and a housing development.

Vancouver (greater metropolitan area population 2,116,000) is the third largest city in Canada. While it tends to have more in common with other large metropolitan areas in other parts of Canada than with smaller urban and rural communities in British Columbia, it also faces some of the same issues that confront other municipalities in the province. In the case of Vancouver, we examined the divestiture of authority over federal property to the Vancouver Fraser Port Authority (VPA).[3] This divestiture privatized the operations of the federally owned Vancouver Port Corporation, but without transferring property title to the City of Vancouver.

The Authority currently has jurisdiction over some 250 kilometers of coastline and 460 hectares of land and is Canada's largest port, handling some 80 million tonnes of cargo in 2006, roughly four times the amount of cargo handled by Montreal, the next largest Canadian port. In 2010, this cargo included the export of pulp, lumber, coal, grain, sulphur, and potash mainly to China, Japan, and South Korea, and the importation of 12 million metric tonnes of cargo from (in descending order) China, the United States, South Korea, Japan, Hong Kong, and Taiwan (Port Metro Vancouver, 2010). The Canada Marine Act (1998) modernized port management and regulations, and promised competitive, efficient, and commercially oriented ports that would benefit Canadian trade and economic development (Transport Canada 2007). Property and land use continue to be dominant policy issues for the VPA as the local Tsawwassen First Nation has overlapping land claims and the provincial Agriculture Land Reserve[4] is adjacent to the Port (Rushe 2008).

Prince George (population 83,000) is located in the central interior of British Columbia. Its labour force is engaged in retail trade, forestry-related industries, education, and health services. Prince George is a hub community for northern British Columbia and services many of the small towns and communities in the region, including a number of First Nations communities. Historically, the city and region have been subject to the vagaries of a boom and bust resource economy. Recently the mountain pine beetle epidemic and the declining housing market in the United States have been causes of great concern regarding the future of the forest industry in the region.

In response to these issues and in an attempt to diversify its economy, both geographically and sectorally, Prince George is currently trying to integrate itself into the APGCI by developing its transportation infrastructure. The Prince George Airport was one of only four airports in British Columbia to be included in the National Airport Strategy and it became part of an overall regional strategy to develop the northern arm of the APGCI. The subsequent expansion of the airport and runway allows cargo planes from Asia to refuel in Prince George. The overall development strategy also includes an inland port to service containers going to and from the Port of Prince Rupert.

Prince Rupert (population 15,000) is located on the west coast of northern British Columbia. Its work force is mostly engaged in forestry- and fishing-related industries, retail trade, tourism, and health services. The opening of a container port in October 2007 has transformed the city and set the stage for future economic development and diversification (Wilson and Summerville 2008). A convergence of factors made the development of a major international container port a reality. Among these were: the opportunities for burgeoning trade with Asia; the federal government's Asia-Pacific Gateway and Trade Corridor Initiative (*Prince Rupert Daily News* 2005); growing congestion at the Vancouver area ports; the relative proximity of Prince Rupert to major Asian ports; spare capacity on road and rail routes to the North American heartland; the deep, natural harbour at Prince Rupert, ideal for container shipping; the growing interest in Alberta for a trade corridor; and the willingness of the Liberal government in British Columbia to support local initiatives.

PERENNIAL ISSUES IN FEDERAL PROPERTY

While the dynamic changes outlined above suggest that the federal government's policies with regards to the divestiture of federal property have paved the way for the economic transformation of some communities, for the most part issues around federal property are perennial and rather mundane. At most, the day-to-day management of federal property has created a series of what one might call bureaucratic intergovernmental exchanges. These involve direct interactions between the federal and municipal government. These interactions are generally one-sided, with the federal government playing the lead role. Occasionally, national or provincial municipal organizations such as the Federation of Canadian Municipalities or the Union of British Columbia Municipalities may step in to lobby the federal government on behalf of their members, but this has not substantially changed intergovernmental dynamics. In our assessment, the provincial government is not involved in the process of managing perennial federal property issues. In the future, provincial bodies such as BC Assessment could become more involved, if the federal government decides to use BC's assessment of property values, but this is currently not the case.

Perhaps the most significant change at the federal level came in 1999 when there was a move to modernize the Municipal Grants Act. This Act was replaced by the Payment in Lieu of Taxes Act, in an effort to represent a fairer and more equitable policy for the "payment." The word "grant" was replaced by "payment" in order "to reflect the federal commitment to pay for the local services it receives" (Jackson 1999). Municipalities cannot tax the federal government, but the policy was meant to ensure that the federal government was paying its fair share to the municipalities and that the municipal (and First Nations') governments had recourse when tenants on federal property defaulted on their taxes.

For the municipalities, the management of real federal property does not seem to be foremost on the agenda. In fact, many local government officials said that they did not have dealings with anyone in particular in the federal government. Local governments have accepted most decisions and worked through their provincial and national associations to voice any concerns. A few issues that were identified during interviews include: a growing concern over board appointments; the need for stronger influence over land use decisions; and the frustration of dealing with the federal bureaucracy. One interviewee said, "[T]he province is very good at sharing the pain and frustration. The provincial bureaucracy may be slow but it is better than at the federal level" (Interview 4). Another municipal leader commented that it appeared as though the federal government was making up its policies with regards to federal property on the spot (Interview 2). As for payments in lieu of taxes, commonly known as PILTs, the interviewee added that the municipality had no control over the federal assessment of the properties' value. Consequently, the municipality takes whatever it can get from the federal government and this, in the interviewee's view, raises issues of fairness (Interview 2). In fact, despite the changes to the legislation and the creation of the PILT Act, the assessment of the value of federal land continues to be an issue.

Another concern that has arisen as a result of the devolution of authority over facilities such as ports and airports to local authorities is the cost of security and fire services. One local official noted that in the case of a small regional airport, the requirement for permanent fire personnel was not possible in a community that only has a volunteer force (Interview 4). The downloading of costs to local authorities has put considerable stress on the limited resources of the local municipalities. This issue is similar for ports, because the RCMP and local police forces are expected to provide port security.

From the perspective of local governments, the main problem with perennial federal property issues is that municipalities seem to have little recourse for action on, or appeal of, federal decisions. Federal government policy has a significant impact on the resources of municipalities. Unfairly assessed properties can lead to significantly lower revenues for local governments. Federal property is exempt from taxation, and federal regulation often increases service costs on those properties. Municipalities, in turn, are left to shoulder these costs on their meager budgets. Municipalities can resort to legal action, as did the City of Montreal against the Montreal Port Authority, but the process is long and costly (*Montreal (City) v. Montreal Port Authority* 2010).

DYNAMIC ISSUES IN FEDERAL PROPERTY

Intergovernmental relations involving all levels of government were most evident in the dynamic federal property issues that arose as a result of significant changes in the way that the federal government managed its property. The federal government's most notable role in this regard was as the initiator of change. The provincial and local governments, on the other hand, reacted to these changes and, along with key social actors, were forced to deal with the consequences of change and the opportunities it presented without much assistance from the federal government. In most cases, federal government decisions that initiated dynamic changes eventually led to positive outcomes. But these largely resulted from the efforts of local governments and actors, with the assistance of the provincial government, rather than from a long-term, visionary policy on the part of the federal government.

Federal Government as Initiator

Before examining the dynamic changes in more detail, it is important to explore the factors which precipitated these changes. As noted by other authors in this book, there were at least two important variables that started the process of policy change in the area of federal property. First, there was a shift in the 1980s to New Public Management (NPM), a model of public administration that blurred the differences between the public and private sectors, integrating aspects of private and business management techniques and the values that underpinned those techniques into the administration of public goods and services (Hood 1991; Inwood 2004). The policy was met with some trepidation as local governments were asked to assume responsibilities that had been the purview of the provincial or federal governments, often without a complementary devolution of funding to pay for these new responsibilities.

At the turn of the century, the province of British Columbia tried to allay these fears by creating the Community Charter. This legislation was supposed to provide more decision-making autonomy for local governments and thus improve the framework for provincial-municipal relations. Passed in 2003, the Charter emerged from a Local Government Bill of Rights, which had been drafted by the Union of British Columbia Municipalities in 1991.[5] Sadly, the

Charter did not provide the resources commensurate with the level of downloaded responsibilities (Long 2009).

The second contextual change was the era of fiscal restraint that began during the 1980s and continued throughout the 1990s. Reductions in program spending by the federal government were a part of an overall strategy to reduce the federal deficit. One could argue that this was the "window of opportunity" for policy changes that would bring about the devolution and divestiture programs. In the area of transportation, for example, the idea of making Canada's transportation system more amenable to needs of an integrated Canadian economy was articulated as early as 1961 by the work of the Macpherson Commission, which "defined the objective of Canada's national transportation policy as the movement of Canadian goods and people with minimum demands on the human and material resources." The Commission recommended that "the transportation policy be achieved through competition rather than regulation, a radical shift from the government's approach for the past 60 years" (Canadian Transportation Agency 2004).

It took a considerable ideological shift in public administration to create the right context for the political will required to make this shift happen. This occurred in the 1980s, when the decline of Keynesianism coincided with the rise of NPM approaches in government. This was reflected in the 1986 Nielsen Task Force, which recommended "changing the machinery of government for managing federal property" and creating a "rigorous program of divestiture of real federal property" (Treasury Board of Canada Secretariat 2004). Significant legislative outcomes of the task force included: the Real Federal Property and Federal Immovables Act (1992); the Payments in Lieu of Taxes Act (2000); the National Airports Plan (1994); the National Marine Policy (1995); and the Canada Marine Act (1998).

This legislative activity led to the federal government divesting authority over and, in some cases, ownership of a number of properties. In the case of airports, the government retained ownership but decided to lease the land to local airport authorities (Transport Canada 2006). In the case of ports, local Canada Port Authorities would be given responsibility for managing ports under local boards of directors with specific knowledge of port administration.[6] In the case of military bases, the policy was to close bases and to sell surplus properties for redevelopment.

Thus, federal policy was designed within the context of fiscal restraint and as part of a shift to the tenets of NPM. A distinction was made between those properties that would come under more local management with new board structures and those that would be sold outright. The federal government appeared to distinguish between property it would keep for the sake of the national interest (ports and larger or geographically strategic airports) and surplus property that it could sell by consolidating services (military bases). However, this two-pronged federal strategy was not designed with the development of property in mind. Although the federal government anticipated that new economic opportunities would emerge from such divestiture, it did not expect or want to play a role in such development, nor did it have a coherent, long-term vision for how the development would take place.

Before examining some of the cases from British Columbia in more detail, it is important to note that it is difficult to speak of intergovernmental relations without mentioning some of the agencies that, while not directly federal, act on behalf of the federal government in the area of federal property. One such agency is the Canada Lands Company (CLC). The CLC appears to have been fairly dormant until the legislation to divest property gave it a considerable role in negotiating post-divestiture land-use. Similarly, Local Port Corporations established under the Canada Ports Corporation Act (1983) were also quiescent bodies until the Canada Marine Act (1998) devolved power and created opportunities for local entrepreneurialism and intergovernmental collaboration. In the wake of the decision to divest property or devolve authority, the federal government often relied on arm's-length agencies to represent its interests in dealing with other levels of government. In the case of the Prince Rupert Port, for example, the federal government had to circumvent its own restrictions on investment, which had been imposed by the Canada Marine Act, and rely on Western Economic Diversification, a federal agency, to provide the $40 million needed to fund the port development (*The Bar-Code Border* 2005). This type of approach was consistent with the principles of NPM: the divestiture of property and authority would lead to eventual redevelopment and the generation of economic growth because private-sector actors and other levels of government would be forced to make the best of a difficult situation by responding to the dynamic changes that had been set in motion. In many cases, however, the process was handled in such a way as to suggest that the federal government lacked any specific vision about the outcomes of these decisions.

An example of this limited and even myopic vision was the federal government's decision to put Prince Rupert's Ridley Coal Terminal up for sale in 2003 (Veniez 2009). The Ridley Coal Terminal had been built in the early 1980s with the expectation that British Columbia would ship large amounts of coal to Asia, but the markets turned down in the 1990s and corporate partners fled. As a result the terminal was viewed as something of a white elephant. After more than a decade of losses, the federal government decided to sell the property to an Ontario firm for less than $3 million (Veniez 2009). The issue was that the terminal was being undervalued: "[t]he price did not represent close to fair value for an asset in which the people of Canada had, by then, invested over $400 million" (Veniez 2009). More importantly, the decision was myopic because the terminal represented an important part of the APGCI. In fact, this was recognized by the Harper government, and as one of his first acts as prime minister, Stephen Harper halted the sale (Veniez 2009). By the mid-2000s, the market had improved dramatically, and the Ridley Coal Terminal became not only financially viable, but also an important part of the Prince Rupert Port Authority and the APGCI. In hindsight, the federal Liberals in 2003 underestimated the potential of the Asian corridor and Canada's natural advantage as a "gateway" to Asia, and only really came on board prior to the 2005 federal election.

Provincial Government

The involvement of the provincial government in the policy process set in motion by dynamic federal property issues was initially reactive and defensive. Decisions concerning federal property were the federal government's to make, and the provincial government was typically forced to react to decisions made unilaterally by Ottawa and with very little consultation. For example, in the case of the federal government's initial decision to close the Canadian Forces Base at Chilliwack, the provincial government reacted negatively, viewing the decision as wrong and short-sighted. In the five years prior to the decision to close the base and consolidate land forces operations in Edmonton, the federal government had spent over $40 million on new infrastructure at the base. Indeed, CFB Chilliwack had just opened new buildings, and had in total 487 buildings valued at $470 million which obviously could not be transported to other bases. As was sharply pointed out, this meant that the taxpayers would be forced to write off these infrastructural investments (Province of British Columbia 1995).

The premier, Mike Harcourt, also pointed out that the decision to close CFB Chilliwack would mean that Canada's third largest province would now be without a land-based military presence. Other urban centres in Canada have major military installations nearby, but Vancouver – located on a seismic fault line and dependent on bridges – would have to rely on Canadian Forces Engineers based in Edmonton to respond to natural disasters. Harcourt added that British Columbia was already shortchanged in federal spending, receiving $700 million less per year than warranted by its population; the Chilliwack decision merely added to this disparity (Province of British Columbia 1995).

Yet, despite this first critical reaction, provincial politicians and government officials soon became more engaged in responding to the new circumstances set in motion by the federal policy. This response may have been in part a consequence of a change in the provincial government after the 2001 election. In the case of the Prince Rupert Port development, one interviewee said that after the BC Liberals came to power, "[t]he province led the charge on development and they did this because they were a bigger player than the local government" (Interview 9). In fact, the interviewee said that in the case of both the container and cruise ship terminals, the provincial government was helpful "in both funding and leadership roles" (Interview 9).

The province played a key role in building the consortium of government and corporate interests behind the Prince Rupert Port development, and has also been a key contributor to redevelopment of the Port of Vancouver. By 2005, the provincial government had already committed more than $1.1 billion towards the infrastructure development for the Asia-Pacific Gateway and Corridor Initiative. Federal promises by 2005 totalled only half that amount, and were not realized until 2006 (Asia Pacific Bulletin 2005).

In the case of Chilliwack, the provincial government has been a key driver of the redevelopment of some former base lands. For example, it provided political and financial support for the creation of the Canada Education Park, including $7.6 million for the

University College of the Fraser Valley (now the University of the Fraser Valley) to purchase thirty-five hectares within the park and another $21.6 million for major renovations of a building on the site (British Columbia 2007). In the case of Prince George, the province also played a leadership and funding role. In September 2007, $11 million was earmarked for the expansion of the airport's runway, so that larger airplanes, including transportation and freight airliners, could land there (Prince George Airport 2007). This money was matched by the federal government (Western Economic Diversification 2007).

Municipal/Regional Government

The response of municipal governments to the policy of devolution and divestiture was similar to that of the provincial government. Municipal governments initially reacted negatively and defensively to the changes, fearing that devolution would encumber them with new responsibilities without providing sufficient resources to pay for them. As it turned out, however, municipal governments, in partnership with other levels of government, created a number of opportunities for local development. Indeed, devolution turned out to be the impetus for a number of important initiatives, including Prince Rupert's port development, the redevelopment of the Vancouver port lands, the Prince George Airport expansion, and the redevelopment of the military base in Chilliwack.

The municipal government in Chilliwack was intimately involved with the redevelopment of the former military base. Although initially opposed to the decision, municipal politicians decided to try to make the best out of a difficult situation. In 2000, a municipal delegation travelled to Ottawa to meet with federal officials in an effort to instigate development on the site. They had some fruitful discussions with Treasury Board officials and made a series of presentations. The municipal government also produced a 400-page briefing paper, a strategy which one interviewee believed made a difference in terms of convincing the federal government to initiate the process of redevelopment after several years of inaction following the initial decision to decommission the base (Interview 2).

In Vancouver, the city and the Vancouver Port Corporation agreed upon a charter to help resolve land use issues, manage municipal services to the port, and coordinate mutual business interests. The charter was signed some six months before the Vancouver Port Authority's Letters Patent were issued in March 1999. It transferred federal property to the Vancouver Port Authority under a leasing agreement. As such, it is clear the City of Vancouver did not resist this change; rather, it anticipated it and looked for opportunities to strengthen community development from the outset. Since then, several other municipalities and even the Tsawwassen First Nation have negotiated charters and memoranda of understanding in order to lay out the ground rules for consultation and negotiation between the different actors involved (Vancouver Port Authority 2004).

In Prince George the transfer of federal lands to the Airport Authority was welcomed and the Airport Authority sought considerable investment for renovations and runway expansion. One municipal interviewee credited collaboration among local authorities such as the Airport Authority and municipal governments for envisioning a larger corridor of development that included coastal and inland ports throughout northern British Columbia and Alberta (Interview 3). The Prince George Airport expansion and the Prince Rupert Port development were part of a greater infrastructure plan for the northern part of the province. The whole strategy of economic development and diversification, particularly in light of the devastating impact of the mountain pine beetle epidemic on the forestry sector and coupled with global trade opportunities with Asia, provided an incentive for governments to work collaboratively. The municipalities involved were able to benefit from the convergence of policy changes – devolution – and the broader changes in the economic and political context.

First Nations: Intergovernmental Actor and Social Force

It is important to note that First Nations in British Columbia are significant actors in the field of federal property, both as governments and as social forces. This chapter distinguishes between the two roles in the following manner. First Nations are part of the intergovernmental matrix when they challenge property divestiture on the grounds that such changes infringe upon their land rights, or when divested properties involve lands that are subject to ongoing treaty negotiations. First Nations are also acting as social forces when they challenge property divestiture in order to secure economic or social benefits related to changes in federal property.

Many of the dynamic federal property issues identified in this chapter triggered a re-examination of Aboriginal rights and title. Since the federal government has a fiduciary duty to consult First Nations, and the treaty negotiation process in so many parts of British Columbia is still underway, divested federal property has been subject to competing and overlapping land claims. Furthermore, it is crucial to note the internal conflicts and divisions which exist within many First Nations in the province. In some cases, these divisions have complicated federal property issues by making it difficult to identify the rightful group with whom the federal and provincial governments need to consult and negotiate. There are a number of band councils, tribal councils, and hereditary chiefs who have made competing assertions regarding their authority to negotiate settlements.

In Chilliwack, the Soowahlie First Nation, whose reserve originally encompassed the military base lands, challenged the decision to transfer the former base lands to the Canada Lands Company in preparation for redevelopment. The First Nations claimed 300 acres of base land that was transferred to the CLC (Morry 2002).[8] In 2000, they were supported by several bands from the Stó:lō Nation, including the Skowkale, Tzeachten, and Yakweakwioose First Nations. The decision was subject to a judicial review and was subsequently appealed to the Federal Court of Appeal in 2001. The Court rejected the appeal, concluding that the band "did not establish that they would suffer irreparable harm from the transfer of subject lands" (*Chief Larry Commodore et al. v. Attorney General of Canada 2001*). Consequently, the Canada Lands Company was allowed to move forward with its development of a residential neighbourhood on the base.

In Vancouver, the Roberts Bank Port Facility of the VPA is located on traditional lands claimed by the Tsawwassen First Nation (TFN). The TFN had taken the federal and provincial governments as well as the VPA to court seeking compensation. In 2004, the TFN and the VPA signed a memorandum which provided for compensation and encouraged development. The TFN eventually signed a treaty with the provincial and federal governments in the summer of 2007.[9] The terms of the agreement included cash settlements and guarantees of employment opportunities at the port. The treaty may also open the door to further port development. Some critics point out that land included in the treaty had been protected by the Agricultural

Land Reserve, an area of land that was previously zoned for agricultural development only. In the 1960s, the provincial government expropriated agricultural lands in order to build a port. In 1973, however, the newly elected NDP government set up the Agricultural Land Reserve (ALR) to protect these lands from development. Under the treaty, the TFN can lease the land to the VPA, at substantially increased value, effectively dedicating agricultural land for industrial use. Since the TFN acts as a governing authority, it can also enter into leasing arrangements with its neighbour, the VPA (Rushe 2008).

In Prince Rupert, the Lax Kwa'laams and Metlaktala First Nations had repeatedly asked the federal government to engage in consultation regarding the container port development. Meaningful consultation on any development that impacts First Nations' traditional territory has become a requirement since the Supreme Court's decision on the Taku River Tlingit case in 2004 (Ritchie 2005). This ruling had very substantial implications in British Columbia where there are few settled treaties. The Lax Kwa'laams and Metlaktala First Nations were not planning to disrupt development but wanted to ensure that prosperity for the city and the region also included prosperity for their communities. Their criticism was directed not so much at the local community and port authority (Ritchie 2005) but rather at the federal government and particularly Jean Lapierre, who had been federal minister of Transport and attorney general. They claimed that they had not been adequately "consulted or accommodated" by the federal government about the port development (Ritchie 2005). By January of 2006, the two First Nations were seeking an injunction on the container terminal project (Ritchie 2005) and local officials were scrambling to push federal officials to deal with the impending crisis.

By mid-2006, with a change in federal government, the Coast Tsimshian Nation, which includes the Lax Kwa'laams and Metlakatla First Nations, were threatening to stop all port development. They were outraged over the lack of consultation. One source reported that "[t]he federal government reportedly admitted it had made a 'boo-boo' in its consultations with Coast Tsimshian about the development of the Fairview Container Terminal in federal court yesterday. They made a 'boo-boo' with respect to the question of the land. So we are hoping that the courts will issue a statutory declaration that will bind the honour of the Crown to come back and consult with the Coast Tsimshian" (Ritchie 2005). Only a few days after the announcement that the Lax Kwa'laams and Metlaktala First Nations had sought an injunction, there was a call by other First Nations in the community to broaden the number of First Nations communities eligible for inclusion in the consultation process. In an article that appeared in the *Prince Rupert Daily News,* Geoff Greenwell, a specialist in Aboriginal affairs in northwestern British Columbia, argued:

> We need to recognize that Aboriginal rights and title belong to individual people, not to band councils ... Band councils were an entity created by the federal government to make it easy to do business with. It is an alien concept to First Nations, it's not a traditional way they govern themselves ... There are a lot of elders, a lot of hereditary chiefs, a lot of land holders and a lot of house chiefs in this area [from] Lax Kwa'laams, Metlakatla and Kitkatla ... all three bands have legitimate claims to the territory due to past use and extensive marriage between the nations. (Vassallo 2006)

The same article pointed out that "[t]he danger otherwise becomes that the government settles with one First Nation and then another arises and makes a similar claim on the land" (Vassallo 2006). And here is the crux of the problem: understanding intergovernmental relations, as it relates to federal property in British Columbia, means understanding the complexity of First Nations politics (Vassallo 2006; Clifton 2006). It is easy to conflate First Nations into one homogeneous group and assume that the consultation process involves First Nations on one side and government (federal and provincial) on the other. The reality, however, is that First Nations in British Columbia are culturally, politically, and economically diverse. Moreover, there are significant disputes within bands about membership, governance, and, most importantly from the perspective of federal property, the issue of development (Vassallo 2006; Clifton 2006).

Social Forces

In this chapter we examine three types of social forces: First Nations, corporate, and citizen-based. As the preceding section noted, First Nations constitute a significant social force, especially when they are seeking to benefit economically and socially from developments connected with the devolution or divestiture of federal property. At the same time, it is important to note that in British Columbia their involvement in the ongoing treaty process has also made them active participants in intergovernmental relations.

Corporate interests, including individual businesses and organizations such as chambers of commerce and local economic development corporations, have been very active in all four communities in federal property matters. Essentially, it is they who have responded in a positive and active way to the opportunities created by dynamic changes in federal property. By contrast, citizen responses to and involvement in these issues have been somewhat muted. Certainly citizen-based actors have been part of the process, but less so than First Nations or corporate actors.

Citizen-based social forces generally mobilize after the divestiture of federal property, when new landholders engage in rezoning or questions of land use emerge. For example, in Prince Rupert there have been some environmental non-governmental organizations that have raised concerns about the impact of port development on the local environment. Similarly, in Vancouver, there has been conflict between the Vancouver Port Authority, the Tsawwassen First Nation, and the agricultural community over land use issues in Delta and Richmond (Rushe 2008). But on the whole, these groups were not significant actors during any stage of the process.[10]

As noted above, First Nations have played an important role as social forces in the debates surrounding the divestiture of federal property. In Prince Rupert, First Nations are concerned about a range of issues set in motion by the divestiture of waterfront property. These include Aboriginal employment at the port and the competing interest of fishers who are concerned about the environmental impacts of port development on the shellfish industry. In an effort to draw attention to these concerns, First Nations groups have mounted a legal challenge to the construction and eventual expansion of the new container port, a decision which has exacerbated tensions between Aboriginal and non-Aboriginal residents in Prince Rupert.

There is also evidence of involvement by quasi-state social forces: that is, institutional interests that rely on government funding but that have a degree of autonomy from government. In Chilliwack, the University College of the Fraser Valley became involved in the land-use planning process for the former CFB lands. With financial assistance from the provincial government, the UCFV acquired 80 acres from the CLC to be used in conjunction with 135 acres of land purchased by the Chilliwack Economic Partners Corporation (CEPCO) to develop the Canada Education Park. In fact, the Canada Education Park is a very good example of a Public-Private Partnership, as it involves the collaboration of governmental agencies such as the provincial Ministry of Advanced Education and the City of Chilliwack and quasi-state actors such as the UCFV, the CEPCO, and the Justice Institute of British Columbia (City of Chilliwack 2003).

It is important to note that the federal property issues in Chilliwack caused the strongest reaction among social forces because the base closure had such broad social impacts on the community. For the most part, in the cases of Prince Rupert and Prince George, the devolution process seems to have been viewed positively, as an opportunity with few if any disadvantages or drawbacks. With the exception of the concerns expressed by First Nations, the changes have been regarded as opportunities from the outset, a perspective that was only achieved much later in Chilliwack. In fact, in Prince Rupert, there seems to be a reluctance to criticize port development for fear of appearing to be against development in a climate where economic growth and diversification are clearly wanted and needed.

POLICY EVALUATION AND CONCLUSIONS

In order to evaluate the federal property policy field, it is necessary to consider the dynamic as separate from the perennial. In terms of the perennial process, one change would be to create a national property management board to assess property values fairly and with municipal input. Such a management board should have an independent appeals process that could settle disputes between the federal and municipal governments over property values. The municipalities want a more transparent and consultative process. The amount of resources required to fight the battle for fair and equitable tax assessments and payments is prohibitive. When asked to give advice to other municipalities dealing with federal property issues, one official quipped, "redraw your municipal boundaries, so you don't have to deal with [federal property issues]" (Interview 2). The official was, of course, joking, but this comment reveals the sense of frustration experienced by many municipal officials when dealing with the federal government.

In this chapter we have focused mainly on the dynamic policies, which are more dramatic and consequential for individual municipalities. As stated earlier, much of what happened in Prince Rupert and Prince George was a convergence of factors that made the federal property devolution policy look prophetic. Clearly the devolution process stimulated an entrepreneurial dynamic in both communities. But governmental collaboration was also encouraged by external factors such as the mountain pine beetle epidemic and the growth of Asian trade. Despite this fortunate outcome, there are still important recommendations to be made.

First, the federal government should scrutinize the policy that limits federal capital investment in properties that have been devolved. Clearly, there continues to be a role for the federal government in investing in projects that have significant national importance. In light of this observation, the second recommendation is that the federal government should reconsider its role in the post–devolution/ divestiture process. Before this process the federal government had too much control, and this appears to have stymied any real collaboration and entrepreneurial spirit, but the post–devolution and divestiture situation is one where the federal government is not participating enough. The federal government needs to embrace the vision of the local communities, where appropriate, and be proactive with more direct collaboration. One municipal official felt that the best way to improve the management and administration of federal property would be to delegate one agency to deal with this policy area (Interview 2). At present, there are too many agencies and interests involved and this complicates the process unnecessarily.

The policy field of federal property in British Columbia is perhaps most uniquely characterized by the active presence and involvement of First Nations governments. No other issue creates such complexity, conflict, and paralysis in the province as does the issue of Aboriginal lands claims and the consultation process. Often, it seems that federal agencies are reluctant to act in areas of federal property because they are afraid that any action will set precedents for future land claim and treaty negotiations. Yet this is precisely the area that needs most attention in order to take advantage of the opportunities that divesture and devolution may present for both Aboriginal and non-Aboriginal communities. Echoing the recommendations of the Progress 250 Report (2002), a report for the BC Progress Board on "Restoring British Columbia's Economic Heartland" states: "The lack of certainty over land use in many areas of the province, coupled with only modest progress in building business-Aboriginal partnerships and concluding modern-day treaties is inhibiting the development of crucial capacity in many Aboriginal communities and is hindering tangible economic development opportunities throughout Region 250" (BC Progress Board 2002).[11]

Still, the VPA experience with the Tsawwassen First Nation shows that progress is possible through careful negotiation. Further, the successful redevelopment of CFB Chilliwack shows how intergovernmental coordination, in conjunction with local social forces, can enable a local community to absorb a severe blow and to rebound creatively. Dynamic federal property issues are contentious and often wrenching, but they can be managed.

NOTES

1 The authors would like to acknowledge the excellent research assistance of Kevin Ginnell and Clarence Hofsink.

2 In Canada, federal real property comprises the real property holdings of the Government of Canada. Federal real property is administered by the Real Property and Materiel Policy Directorate of the Treasury Board of Canada. See http://www.tbs-sct.gc.ca/dfrp-rbif/home-accueil-eng.aspx.

3 The Vancouver Fraser Port Authority changed its name on 19 June 2008 to the Port Metro Vancouver. For the purpose of this chapter we will use The Vancouver Port Authority (VPA).

4 British Columbia's Agricultural Land Reserve (ALR) was established between 1974 and 1976 by BC Land Commission. It consists of a social land use zone and was intended to protect the province's diminishing supply of agricultural land. See http://www.alc.gov.bc.ca/alr/Establishing_the_ALR.htm.

5 The Charter was designed to strengthen municipal capacity to make local decisions and be held accountable for them, protect municipalities from provincial downloading, and clarify provincial-municipal relations. See http://www2.news.gov.bc.ca/nrm_news_releases/2003MCAWS0033-000250-Attachment1.htm and http://www.cserv.gov.bc.ca/lgd/gov_structure/community_charter/index.htm.

6 From the Canada Marine Act: "The directors of a port authority appointed under paragraph 14(1)d) shall have generally acknowledged and accepted stature within the transportation industry or the business

community and relevant knowledge and extensive experience related to the management of a business, to the operation of a port or to maritime trade" (Transport Canada 2007).

7 There are a number of sources that demonstrate the angst over the government's failure to support a gateway strategy, including: Asia Pacific Bulletin #237, 30 November 2005 (http://www.asiapacificbusiness.ca/apbn/pdfs/bulletin237.pdf); "Prime Minister Harper Launches Asia-Pacific Gateway and Corridor Initiative," 11 October 2006 (http://www.pm.gc.ca/eng/media.asp?category=1&id=1352); "Campbell Selling Pacific Dream on His Tour of Asia: Premier in China to Share His Vision of Massive Ports on B.C.'s West Coast," *Prince Rupert Daily News*, 21 November 2006.

8 Although they had reached Stage 4 of the treaty process by the mid-1990s, they have not participated in treaty negotiation since the creation of the Stó:lō Tribal Council in 1995 (British Columbia 2007b).

9 Tsawwassen First Nation and the Vancouver Port Authority Roberts Bank Development Memorandum of Agreement.

10 It is important to note that some of these issues are still evolving and that citizen groups could play a more active role in future deliberations about the properties in question.

11 Region 250 represents the BC telephone area code for places outside Vancouver.

INTERVIEWS

1 Prince George, October 2007.
2 Chilliwack, May 2007.
3 Chilliwack, May 2007.
4 Prince George, October 2007.
5 Prince George, October 2007.
6 Prince George, October 2006.
7 Prince George, October 2006.
8 Prince George, October 2006.
9 Prince Rupert, October 2007.

REFERENCES

Asia Pacific Bulletin. 2005. "When a Pause Is Not a Problem." 30 November. http://www.asiapacificbusiness.ca/apbn/pdfs/bulletin237.pdf.

The Bar-Code Border. 2005. "Skinning the Cat at Prince Rupert: How Ottawa Skirts Law for New Container Corridor." Vol. 2., no. 52: 1–3.

BC Assessment. 2008. "Factsheet: Real Property Assessment and Taxation in British Columbia." March. http://www.bcassessment.bc.ca/pdf/publications/fact_sheets/FS15_Amalg_Real_Prop_Assmt_Hist.pdf.

BC Progress Board. 2002. "Restoring British Columbia's Economic Heartland." http://www.bcprogressboard.com/2002Report/RestoreBCEH.pdf.

British Columbia. 2007. "Premier Announces $29M for UCFV Campus, Trades Facility." Ministry of Advanced Education and Labour Market Development, 16 January. http://www.aved.gov.bc.ca/photogallery/coell/ucfv_campus.htm.

– 2007b. "Stó:lō Tribal Council." Ministry of Aboriginal Relations and Reconciliation. http://www.gov.bc.ca/arr/firstnation/stolo_tribal/default.html.

Canadian Transportation Agency. 2004. "100 Years at the Heart of Transportation – An Historical Perspective." http://www.cta-otc.gc.ca/about-nous/centennial/rpt/2_e.html#_ednref16.

Chief Larry Commodore et al. v. Attorney General of Canada, [2001] F.C. 387. http://decisions.fca-caf.gc.ca/en/2001/2001fca387/2001fca387.html.

City of Chilliwack. 2003. "Institutes Take Giant Step on Education Park Governments, UCFV, Justice Proposal." 25 July. http://www.chilliwack.com/main/page.cfm?id=12&prid=107&prsearchshow=details#.

Clifton, Nancy. 2006. "Help Individuals, Not Bands." *Prince Rupert Daily News*, 28 August.

Hood, C. 1991. "A Public Management for All Seasons?" *Public Administration* 69, no. 1: 3–19.

Inwood, Gregory J. 2004. *Understanding Canadian Public Administration*. Toronto: Pearson.

Jackson, Anthony. 1999. Bill C-10: An Act to Amend the Municipal Grants Act. Public Works Canada, Economics Division. http://dsp-psd.pwgsc.gc.ca/Collection-r/LoPBdP/LS/362/c10-e.htm.

Long, Robert. 2009. "British Columbia's Community Charters: Home Rule or More Paternalism?" MA Thesis. Prince George BC: University of Northern British Columbia.

Montreal (City) v. Montreal Port Authority. [2010] SCC 14. http://csc.lexum.umontreal.ca/en/2010/2010scc14/2010scc14.html.

Morry, Lisa. 2002. "CFB Land Grab Angers Chief: Soowahlie Band Never Notified of Change in Plans for 300 Acres." *Chilliwack Times* 2, no. 7.

Prince George Airport. 2007. "Province Provides $11 Million for PG Airport Expansion." 21 September. http://www.pgairport.ca/yxs/media/press_releases/index.php?cat=1&pr=18.

Prince Rupert Daily News. 2005."Ottawa Finds $590m to Boost Trade through B.C." 21 October.

Ritchie, Leanne. 2005. "First Nations Call on Feds to Discuss Port." *Prince Rupert Daily News*, 5 October.

Rushe, Ronan. 2008. "Landmark Land Decision." *Canadian Geographic*. April. http://www.canadiangeographic.ca/Magazine/apro8/indepth/ steves.asp?comments=all.

Transport Canada. 2007. *Canada Marine Act*. http://www.tc.gc.ca/acts-regulations/GENERAL/c/cma/act/cma-a.html.

– 2006. "Airport and Port Programs – Airports National Airports Policy." http://www.tc.gc.ca/programs/airports/policy/nap/NAP.htm.

Treasury Board of Canada Secretariat. 2004. "Understanding Federal Real Property Management." June. http://www.tbs-sct.gc.ca/rpm-gbi/rpmd-pubs/frpm01_e.asp.

Vancouver Port Authority. 2006. "Statistics Overview 2006." http://www.portvancouver.com/statistics/docs/2006_Statistics_Overview.pdf.

– 2004. *Memorandum of Agreement with the Tsawwassen First Nation*. http://www.tsawwassenfirstnation.com/TFN_VPA_Memorandum_of_Agreement.pdf.

Vassallo, James. 2006. "'Summit' Called For to Solve Port Issues." *Prince Rupert Daily News*, 25 January.

Veniez, Daniel D. 2009. "A Terminal Sale: Ridley Terminals Must Be Privatized in the Manner that Best Serves Western Canadian Coal Producers." *National Post,* 21 May. http://network.nationalpost.com/np/blogs/fpcomment/archive/2009/05/21/a-terminal-sale.aspx.

Western Economic Diversification. 2007. "Canada's New Government Finalizes $11 Million Contribution Agreement for Prince George Airport." 21 September. http://www.wd.gc.ca/eng/77_9582.asp.

Wilson, Gary N., and Tracy Summerville. 2008. "Transformation, Transportation or Speculation? The Prince Rupert Container Port and Its Impact on Northern British Columbia." *Canadian Political Science Review* 2, no. 4: 26–39.

3

Federal Land Transfers in New Brunswick

KURT PEACOCK AND ROBERT MacKINNON

From post offices, lighthouses, and wharves, to railways, ports, airports, and military bases, federal land holdings are a significant presence in New Brunswick's provincial landscape. According to the Treasury Board's online registry, the province of New Brunswick has 1,109 federally owned properties on 185,000 hectares within its boundaries. This represents nearly five percent of 24,007 federal properties across Canada and less than half a percent of the area of all federal lands (Treasury Board 2010). By comparison, New Brunswick's population at the 2006 census, of just fewer than 750,000, represents just over two percent of Canada's total population (Statistics Canada 2006). Federal property is present in virtually every region of New Brunswick. Thus, federal lands and their use remain a relevant issue for government officials and citizens alike.

In many instances, the divestiture of federal property in New Brunswick occurs within close proximity to many New Brunswickers and often becomes an issue of local and regional concern. Initially, local interest is focused on the loss of federal investment in the region, and the associated potential job losses. Later on, as the divestiture process evolves, community interests shift focus to the potential reuse of the federal land, and the perceived benefits for the municipality, region, and province. Political champions for the potential reuse of surplus federal lands may be found at all three levels of government. Once a federal property is deemed surplus, the divestiture process follows a standard procedure involving a chain of federal bidders prior to the property being offered to the municipality or to the public. The chain of potential bidders includes federal departments (other than the one that is disposing of the land), agent Crown corporations, the provincial government, and finally, the municipality (Treasury Board 2009). This process is similar to that found in other provinces.

Federal lands are held by a wide range of different ministries, agencies, and commissions; and while the Treasury Board establishes uniform protocols for land use policies and property transfers, there are often profound differences between the way different government departments interact with their host communities over assets that are ultimately owned by the people of Canada. In some cases, government departments can have significantly different land use policies influencing the same municipality. For example, in Saint John, the Department of National Defence (DND) lobbied to have an old military barracks, built before the Great Fire of 1877, placed under the city's heritage protection by-law prior to its eventual sale as surplus property (Saint John 2009). This small measure, which resulted in a spot amendment to the municipal heritage by-law, placed a significant federal building under permanent local heritage protection while at the same time facilitating its renewal as commercial office space. Across the Saint John Harbour, within view of the renewed heritage complex, Transport Canada allowed Partridge Island, a national historic site, to suffer from vandalism and neglect, fenced off from tourists and local residents alike. These differing federal approaches to significant property highlight how important federal holdings located within close proximity in the same community can be subjected to vastly different policies.

Given New Brunswick's relatively small population, its significant number of elected officials (ten MPs, fifty-five MLAs, and hundreds of local municipal officials), and its history of "boom-bust" resource industries, questions of economic development and local political influence are often bound up with the divestiture of federal lands. In many parts of the province, government employment linked to federal lands has long been of more concern to local officials and politicians than the property itself. Relative to its population, New Brunswick has comparatively more provincial and federal employees than elsewhere in Canada. According to Statistics Canada, roughly one in four employed New Brunswickers draws a government paycheque (Statistics Canada 2009). Throughout most of the province's history, the state has been seen not only as a guardian of the public trust, but as the principal driving force for the economy. A Hatfield-era report in the early 1970s summed up the provincial labour market: "the public sector represents the major industrial employer of labour in the Province ... New Brunswick thus has an above average dependency on governmental activity as a source of jobs" (NB Economic Advisor 1973, 3).

Predictably, local business interests have historically lobbied for more federal jobs, and their associated local purchasing power. When the Canadian Forces Base Oromocto was planned in the early 1950s, it was officially welcomed as an economic stimulus for all of New Brunswick; however, competing mercantile groups from Fredericton and Saint John quickly turned their attention to attracting the base's administrative headquarters. Saint John sought to have the base's headquarters located in Welsford, at the southern tip of the extensive training site and relatively close to the port city. Fredericton, on the other hand, promoted the municipality of Oromocto, located just outside of the provincial capital, as the headquarters' site. With its sitting federal cabinet minister in the St Laurent government (former UNB president Milton Gregg), Fredericton won the day.

This pattern of political influence on federal property decisions has been repeated on numerous occasions across New Brunswick. Often, key public policy decisions surrounding seaport or airport investments, federal customer contact centres, and military bases can be influenced by partisan strategy involving either New Brunswick's regional federal minister or the provincial governing party in Fredericton. Some critics of regional development in the Maritimes, such as the Halifax-based Atlantic Institute for Market Studies (AIMS), have suggested that there is a strong correlation between federal investments in the region (through influential agencies such as the Atlantic Canada Opportunities Agency) and the government's need to appease its supporters among members of Parliament (Savoie 2006, 189–92). This is not simply a New Brunswick phenomenon, as regionalism and the presence of regional chieftains within the Canadian parliamentary system have a long tradition. It nonetheless highlights how political pressure can influence public policy surrounding federal lands in a province that has only recently seen its unemployment rate dip below double digits. Local actors (be they municipal mayors or business sector lobbies) certainly play a role, but their influence is often minor compared either to economic development officials attached to the provincial or federal governments, or to the elected provincial and federal representatives who routinely turn job creation into New Brunswick's holy grail. In most parts of the province, the federal lands themselves are treated as a secondary consideration, well behind the critical questions of economic security and employment. Only in the larger centres, where land values themselves create a degree of scarcity, are land use conflicts readily apparent.

This chapter addresses federal land use issues in New Brunswick by examining several case studies of important federal land use issues that have had significant implications for three of New Brunswick's urban centres (Saint John, Moncton, and Fredericton), and for the province as a whole. These cases highlight the unique relations between cities and the federal government when a province does not have a dominant metropolis. The chapter will also examine the closing of the Canadian Forces Base in Chatham, an event which highlights the unique challenges rural New Brunswick faces when the federal government divests key land holdings. It will first examine the divergent community responses to the closings of CFB Chatham and the Canadian National Railway Shops in Moncton (CN Shops), before turning to several land use conflicts involving the Port of Saint John, and airport devolution in the City of Fredericton. The conclusion suggests lessons that the New Brunswick experience may offer policy-makers who seek to improve how Ottawa manages its land assets on the nation's periphery, well removed from the mandarins of the Treasury Board or Public Works.

FROM CFB CHATHAM TO SKY PARK MIRAMICHI

Canadian Forces Base Chatham was located in northeastern New Brunswick in the former Town of Chatham (now part of the amalgamated City of Miramichi). The base provided one of the key employment centres in this small rural community, which for most of its history relied on paper and forest products as its economic base.

When the federal government announced the closure of CFB Chatham in 1994, the Town of Chatham was conditioned to expect severe economic challenges from the loss of many armed forces personnel. In fact, senior Ottawa officials had alluded to the closure of the base several years earlier. It was only through constant and consistent lobbying on the part of the local chamber of commerce and regional politicians that the base continued to operate through to its final years. A 1989 history of the Chatham Airfield highlighted this uncertainty, tersely concluding: "the final structuring of the base is indeed unsettled" (Less 1989, 102).

The potential closure of this air base, which was once home to the CF 101 Voodoo fighter squadron, loomed large over local politics and the community's economy for much of the 1980s. While the base facilities, including highly valued recreational buildings such as the in-ground pool, were considered community assets, it was the economic security provided by employment at the base that was of paramount concern to local residents. Of the 6,700 residents of Chatham in 1979, more than 1,100 were employed at the air base. This employment contributed over \$25 million in payroll and procurements to the local and regional economy (Miramichi Regional Development Corporation 1979). Local entrepreneurs fretted over the potential loss of these dollars. "If the air force goes down, it'll finish Chatham. It'd ruin the whole damn economy," warned John Creagan, a longtime Chatham haberdasher, in a 1981 newspaper interview. "You take 27 million out of the Miramichi and it's like taking a billion out of Toronto or Montreal" (*Moncton Times* 1981).

Given CFB Chatham's economic clout within the Miramichi's regional economy, politicians at all levels were careful to respond to community concerns over the future of CFB Chatham. As early as 1981, Defence Minister Gilles LaMontagne pledged, "the obligation that the federal government is accepting now is to assist this community in making the transition to a new condition in which life will no longer revolve around the existence of a fighter squadron, and, if possible, to even turn the situation into an economic opportunity" (*Northumberland News* 1981). The community, in turn, mobilized various social and economic actors against any potential base closure. In the spring of 1982, an estimated 7,000 people took part in a march on CFB Chatham, with representatives from organized labour, the regional economic development corporation, and the local business community joining Premier Hatfield in the protest. One Miramichi newspaper reported that at least 16,000 letters concerning the future of CFB Chatham were sent to Prime Minister Trudeau in 1982 (*Miramichi Weekend* 1982). A promising future for the base formed part of Premier Hatfield's 1982 re-election platform, with the governing provincial Tories envisioning flight simulators, a helicopter industry, and a nuclear training centre at the site.

During the fall election campaign, Premier Hatfield warned that the "federal government's solution [towards possible base closure] would not satisfactorily fill the potential and needs of the Miramichi" (*Evening Times Globe* 1982). Hatfield's partisan gambit failed to produce local electoral support, as Chatham constituents voted for a young Liberal lawyer named Frank McKenna in 1982 rather than the governing Tories. The community mobilization, however, did send a message to officials in Ottawa. After his election as prime minister, Brian Mulroney (who spent time in Chatham as a boarding student at St Thomas College in the 1950s) pledged to the Chatham mayor that the base would remain open for as long as he was in office (Interview 6).[1]

With the election of Jean Chretien's Liberals in Ottawa in 1993, deficit fighting became the paramount focus of federal public policy, with the Department of National Defence being one of the first ministries to face severe budget cuts. In Paul Martin's first budget, CFB Chatham was one of several bases targeted for closure. The fallout was felt immediately by the community, and by Chatham's MLA, Premier Frank McKenna. Rising in the provincial legislature, McKenna highlighted in deeply personal terms how years of battling over the future of the base had placed significant burdens on the community:

I want to speak specifically to the people of Chatham and speak to them as an MLA, rather than as Premier. I have had the privilege of serving that community for a dozen years now, and together with the people of Chatham, I have spent a quarter of my entire life fighting to retain the jobs at CFB Chatham. As somebody in our delegation recently noted, "We won every battle, but we lost the war" ... People on the Miramichi have lived with that insecurity for over a dozen years, and it has been like a cloud hanging over the economic head of all Miramichiers. It has affected our development, it has certainly stunted our confidence and it has influenced our view of ourselves. What the Miramichi needed was certainty, the certainty of a future and the certainty of a direction. The certainty I had hoped for was the certainty that we would continue in perpetuity to maintain a federal presence in our community ... In my town, [the base] is not only the biggest employer but virtually the only employer. The people of the Miramichi have deserved better direction and better certainty than they have had for a long, long time. (NB Hansard 1994)

Premier McKenna concluded by pledging that job creation would be the focus of all efforts related to the closing of CFB Chatham; the actual base property and its assets were merely an afterthought: "We will get on with replacing that economic activity with other economic activity, which will guarantee a future for the community" (NB Hansard 1994). The leader of the provincial opposition did consider the question of federal defence holdings in New Brunswick, but only through the controversial lens of national unity. Danny Cameron, leader of the short-lived Confederation of Regions Party, whose platform was focused on opposition to official bilingualism, asked rhetorically: "I wonder how long it will be before Camp Gagetown is moved to the province of Quebec?" (NB Hansard 1994).

In the years between the 1994 announcement and the eventual transfer of base assets to the province in 1997, Chatham struggled to develop a satisfactory economic renewal plan. Chatham business interests dominated the local "save-our-base" committee, which had been meeting informally since the early 1980s. It was subsequently restructured and developed a business plan for base reuse. The community had the full support of the New Brunswick government in this task, as Premier McKenna ensured that senior economic development officials were linked into any and all plans concerning the CFB Chatham site. By 1996, a formal proposal to turn the base site into Sky Park Miramichi, a multi-use business park with close ties to the provincial department of economic development, was presented to the Atlantic Canada Opportunities Agency (ACOA). The report argued that the "solution to this issue [of base closure] should not be or become a burden to local tax payers" and called for a "prudent, deliberate and objective assessment of CFB Chatham ... which could provide for the viable redevelopment of base assets as well as other initiatives in support of local economic development" (Sky Park Miramichi 1996). The federal Department of Defence transferred the base site to the province for one dollar in April 1997, and the ACOA provided over $10 million in economic assistance for the redevelopment project.

The flurry of official announcements over the next few years certainly implied that the transformation of CFB Chatham into Sky Park Miramichi was going to be "an unqualified success," as the title of a 1998 promotional brochure described it (Sky Park Miramichi 1998). "The determination of the people of the Miramichi to overcome adversity is an example for all New Brunswickers," Premier

Camille Theriault (McKenna's successor) said in 1999. "Sky Park Miramichi is a model of economic redevelopment and diversification, and we are proud to have been able to play a part in this success" (NB Economic Development 1999). Within three years of the base transfer, provincial government officials claimed that over 750 jobs had been created (NB Economic Development 1999).

While small private-sector manufacturing activity did locate in the Sky Park complex, and these jobs were welcomed by a community suffering under a prolonged forestry downturn, this employment has yet to fully make up for the loss of so many armed forces personnel. A key tenant of the base site, the industrial firm Atcon, went into receivership in 2009 despite generous financial support from the provincial government.

While the private sector has not filled the void left by CFB Chatham, in place of the lost defence jobs there has been a clustering of smaller government agencies offering employment opportunities. These have included a new provincial youth detention centre opened in 1998 at the edge of the base, a federal employment insurance contact centre, and a controversial contact centre tasked with maintaining the national gun registry (the two latter centres were located in Chatham's downtown, a few kilometers north of the base site). The housing quarters once utilized by military personnel were marketed as an affordable site for retirement living; the business plan for "Retirement Miramichi" was based partly on a similar plan designed for Elliot Lake, Ontario.

Chatham ceased to exist as a separate municipality, in part, because of the base closure. With the loss of its major employer, the cost of maintaining municipal services had become a serious concern. A sympathetic provincial report, issued two months after the closure of CFB Chatham was first announced, called for regional amalgamation of Chatham, Newcastle, and surrounding communities into a new city of Miramichi. Observing that "the area suffers from over governance, having five municipal councils and 33 elected officials," the report argued that amalgamation was in many ways an extension of the methods in which community leaders "represent the area in a common cause ... in collectively developing plans for minimizing anticipated losses through the announced closure of CFB Chatham" (NB Municipal Affairs 1994). Both the base pool and the fire station were eventually transferred to the new City of Miramichi.

More than a decade after the official (and hopeful) opening of Sky Park Miramichi, the site remains an important community asset. Yet shifting economic forces have caused much of the site's potential to remain undeveloped. The air strip, which once hosted daily commercial flights to Montreal and was highlighted as a key locational advantage in attracting new export-ready business interests, now has virtually no commercial activity. Enterprise Miramichi, in a brief to the 2007 Task Force on New Brunswick Self-Sufficiency, expressed the business community's frustration. "The Miramichi airport has the longest runway in Atlantic Canada (10,000 feet). [It is] being underutilized and this is a serious waste of valuable infrastructure" (Enterprise Miramichi 2007, 9). Chatham's downtown, whose merchants feared the worst as far back as 1981, recently started to dismantle some of its traffic lights due to a lack of vehicle activity. Former Chatham mayor Rupert Bernard, who served as Sky Park Miramichi's initial chair (and still serves on municipal council) is philosophical over the closing of the base, and the effect it had on the former town of Chatham. "The community effort that went into this [base conversion] was unbelievable," noted Bernard. "At the end of the day, we felt we replaced what we lost, but didn't move one step ahead" (Interview 6).

The closure of CFB Chatham highlighted the lack of political and economic clout that the Miramichi community faced, as their campaign for economic renewal took place far from the centre with its political and economic decision-makers. "DND in particular were extremely difficult to deal with," said Bernard. "At one point, they were threatening to bulldoze the base." The community looked with a certain envy at other Maritime communities which bounced back from base closings, including Summerside, PEI, which received a GST collection centre, millions of dollars in economic development funds, and the keys to base assets as part of its 1988 closure. "We surrendered far too late," said Bernard. "In 1988, the federal government still thought they had money. In 1994, the cupboard was bare."

MONCTON'S CN LANDS: FROM SHOP YARDS TO PARKLAND

In much the same way that CFB Chatham was the principal employer in the town of Chatham, the Canadian National Railway's Shop Yards (CN Shops) served as Moncton's major employer for nearly a century. The closure of the CN Shops in 1988 and the abandonment of the site by Canadian National in 1990 were considered serious calamities by local community groups and public officials. As in Chatham, the closing of the CN Shops, where many of the locomotives used across eastern Canada were maintained, was publicly discussed well in advance of the closure. Again, the greatest community concern was the expected loss of employment. The *Moncton Times Transcript*, for example, reported on rumours of an anticipated closure in 1985. Moncton's mayor at the time, George Rideout, recalled the "fights and agonies" of twenty years earlier, when his parents, who had served sequentially as members of Parliament for the city of Moncton, fought to keep the city's shop yard open (*Moncton Times Transcript* 1986). Given that the CN Shops employed approximately a thousand workers throughout much of its final decade, there were vehement protests against the announced closure. Once Canadian National ceased its local Moncton operations in 1988, one of the jobs lost was that of the Conservative member of Parliament, Dennis Cochrane, who fell to the Liberal nominee, former mayor George Rideout.

Less discussed, however, were the environmental impacts of nearly a century of industrial operations. As New Brunswick journalist, David Stonehouse, eventually described it for *Maclean's Magazine*, "the closure threw several thousand people out of work and left an environmental mess just a 20 minute walk from city hall: petroleum waste, arsenic, copper, lead and zinc. It was a blight, plain and simple" (*Maclean's* 2003). A massive remediation effort had to be undertaken before many parts of this site could be reused. The Canada Lands Company (CLC), the Crown corporation tasked with the disposal of the former CN properties, has actively rehabilitated this property. Some of the statistics on this transformational project reflect the challenges that were faced: 4,000 tons of metal recycled, 120,000 tons of lead contamination removed, 30,000 tons of wood, formerly used in shop operations, chipped for reuse on the site, and many kilometers of drainage and irrigation pipes installed. Still, this massive remediation project came in ahead of time and under budget. Consequently, it received an Award of Excellence for the comprehensive environmental remediation program at the Moncton railway yards (Canada Lands Company 1999, 7).

Given both the economic and environmental challenges that the closure of the CN Shops created, it is somewhat surprising to see how successful the former industrial site has become. The seventy-eight-hectare site of the former CN Shops is currently occupied by a massive public commons space, incorporating over a dozen soccer and ball fields and a four-plex ice rink; it also houses a small technology park that has incorporated Leadership in Energy and Environmental Design (LEED) principles in its construction, and a housing subdivision that has been heavily influenced by high-density "new urbanism" principles.[2] As a result of this massive transformation, the former CN Shops lands have been highlighted as a successful case study in a number of presentations and promotional videos prepared by the CLC (Canada Lands Company 2003).

How did this particular former federal property turn into a vibrant community asset, while other New Brunswick properties, be they the old CFB Chatham runway or the immigration facilities on Partridge Island in Saint John, remain underdeveloped? Former CN workers seemed to be among the most intrigued by this question. "This land sat barren for so many years," former shop worker Bob McIsaac told *Maclean's Magazine* in 2003. "I never dreamed we would have anything like this – it's just phenomenal." There were many reasons why the revitalization of the former CN Shop Yards succeeded, including strategic municipal interventions, better-than-expected environmental conditions, and a central urban location. Because the shops were situated within close proximity of Moncton's Central Business District (CBD), the potential for redeveloping the site was immediately apparent to civic boosters and city residents.

Those who had grand schemes in mind for the revitalization of the former CN Shop Yards were certainly assisted by prevailing economic conditions. While broad economic forces hampered those involved with "Sky Park Miramichi" as they sought to replace the loss of more than a thousand jobs due to the closure of the Chatham air base, the initial economic concern over the closing of Moncton's CN Yards gradually dissipated in the face of fairly constant labour force growth in the city. Rural-to-urban migration from northern New Brunswick brought a stream of young, bilingual workers to Moncton just as older industrial employers (such as the CN Shops) went into decline. New information technologies and a robust linkage between NB Tel (the former provincial telecom) and provincial economic development officials ensured that Moncton would play a role in the explosion of telecommunications industries emerging across North America in the 1990s. The resulting growth in local call-centre operations (many of which had sizeable bilingual staffs) "added nearly 2,000 jobs to the local economy, almost making up for those [jobs] lost when the rail yard shut down." This was the conclusion of a 1994 *New York Times* article, entitled "The Moncton Miracle," which marveled at Moncton's swift economic rebound (*New York Times* 1994). Other white-collar employers, such as Blue Cross Atlantic and the Atlantic Canada Opportunities Agency (ACOA), also contributed to the economic diversification of Moncton, mitigating the financial blow initially caused by the CN Shop Yards closure. Member of Parliament Brian Murphy, who had served previously as Moncton's mayor, believes that this rapid labour force transformation helped ensure that the negative economic impacts of the CN Shops closure were minimized: "If Moncton had been Chatham ... if it had been a unilingual, non-central entity, the closing of the shops might have killed Moncton" (Interview 2).

Brian Murphy, as Moncton's mayor and later its member of Parliament, played a key role in turning a large parcel of former industrial land into a multi-use recreational complex and park. This illustrates how, in a small province, one public official can move a relatively complex file forward. He was certainly helped by mandarin support – a dedicated team of officials at the Canada Lands Company who were anxious to revitalize this brownfield site assisted Murphy. Additional support came from then–Moncton MP and federal cabinet minister Claudette Bradshaw. She was able to use her influence to help loosen bureaucratic logjams. In contrast, Murphy found that the provincial government, at that time led by Conservative premier and Moncton-area MLA Bernard Lord, was largely uninvolved with the reclamation project (with the exception of select environmental approvals). Even with these other influences, the ultimate success in turning the CN Shops into a significant community asset rested with Moncton's city hall. The city was facing community pressure to expand its recreational assets; thus, it saw the former CN Shops site as a way to address this challenge and, in the process, improve the city's quality of life. "We were given an opportunity – a right of first refusal – and we took it," noted Murphy. "There is no business case for what we did. The return on investment is smiling kids" (Interview 2).

In the Moncton Rail Yards case, success in the reuse of federal lands was largely a result of dedicated federal and local politicians, who were supported by staff at Canada Lands. An effective vision was created and followed through by all concerned. The generally upbeat local economy in this bilingual city helped drive the project as success could be seen from a continually growing labour force, albeit in a different sector. The CN Shop Lands reclamation is still used by Moncton politicians as an example of the community's ability to continuously adapt, and to become, in the process, one of the region's most dynamic urban economies.

FROM WORKING PORT TO RECREATIONAL DESTINATION: LAND USE CONFLICTS IN SAINT JOHN'S INNER HARBOUR

Saint John, New Brunswick's most industrial city, has been the site of animated discussions over the divestiture and use of federal land. The inner harbour, which has always been a key link between the provincial economy and global trading partners, is largely made up of parcels of federal land managed by the Saint John Port Authority, one of eighteen Canadian Port Authorities established and governed by the Canada Marine Act of 1998 (CMA) (Dion et al. 2002, 188). Smaller parcels of land in Saint John's city centre are owned by the Department of National Defence (the old Armoury), Transport Canada (Partridge Island), the Department of Fisheries and Oceans (the Coast Guard site), and Revenue Canada (the old Customs Building). In recent years, much of this property has been of interest to municipal officials who have been promoting the revitalization of the city's uptown core. At the same time, these federal lands (particularly those involved in port operations) have been considered key components of the provincial economy, as well as of national interest. While the community has generally embraced the federal presence in Saint John, the city is less reliant on federal employment than other New Brunswick communities (Moncton, for instance, has three times as many federal government employees). For much of the last decade, specific parcels of federal land, and not the employees that worked there, have been emerging as the foci of the city's new urban vision.

Before addressing some of the contemporary questions surrounding federal lands in Saint John, it is necessary to provide some historical context, particularly with respect to the port lands. In the nineteenth century era of "wood, wind and sail," Saint John's harbour was one of the most prosperous in North America (Acheson

1985, 5; Wynn 1981).[3] However, as steel-hulled vessels became more common, the competitive advantages associated with plentiful timber supplies weakened, and the harbour's economic might shrank. Federal trade policy also played a significant role. The mercantile elite of Saint John were often envious of Canadian exports sent by rail to Portland, Maine, rather than through their local port; and by the earliest decades of the twentieth century they were outright jealous of their Maritime competitor, Halifax. As Elizabeth McGahan notes, "Competition with Halifax within a national context for winter port status [had] resulted in a sobering realization of the position of the port within the transport hierarchy" (1977, 76).[4] Not surprisingly, a key demand of local activists who championed the Maritime Rights movement in the 1920s was increased federal assistance for the Port of Saint John (Forbes 1977).

The opening of the St Lawrence Seaway created another serious economic challenge for the Port of Saint John. The presence of a shipping route that led to the central industrial heart of the North American continent severely undermined Saint John's winter port status, while the growth of container ship traffic was constrained by the relatively narrow inner harbour. In 1976, George Nader's *Profiles of Fifteen Metropolitan Centres* predicted that, for Saint John, "future prospects remain bleak and the city's continued growth will inevitably depend on the forging of a new role for its port" (Nader 1976, 63). Thus, an industrial plan for the city drafted in the 1970s recommended moving a sizeable part of the port's operations into much deeper water, outside the inner harbour. While the port eventually achieved some success in attracting container traffic to the west side of the harbour, the more ambitious planned deep-water expansion never achieved its anticipated levels (Wallace 1975, 438–41).

Over the last three decades, changes in national ports' policies also had a dramatic effect on the port's development due to changing patterns of international trade. Commencing in the 1980s, Ottawa promoted a more decentralized governance structure for national port operations under the Canada Port Corporation Act of 1983. With loosened ties to the federal government came less regular financial support. As the twentieth century closed, the Port of Saint John, like other Canadian Port Authorities operating under the Canada Marine Act, was expected to be largely self-sufficient (Ircha 1999; Ircha 2002). At the same time, long-term shipping from Russia and Japan appeared less frequently in the harbour, and Saint John port officials were forced to look for new sources of revenue. Throughout the 1990s, changes to the harbour's skyline highlighted Saint John's economic transition. The port's grain elevators (which had been under-utilized for decades), were torn down, as was the west-side passenger immigration station building. The Canadian Pacific Railway, which had linked the port of Saint John to central Canada since the nineteenth century, was sold off to local interests. Replacing these older vestiges of commercial activity came new sources of revenue, in the form of cruise ships. Although bulk commodity shipments, most notably crude oil and potash, continued to play a significant role in the daily life of the port, overall, Saint John's inner harbour has seen far fewer ships than in past decades. In 1977, for example, the port of Saint John moved over a million tons of container cargo; by 2008, this number had dropped to a little over 300,000 tons (Saint John Port Authority 1978; Saint John Port Authority 2009).

Since both potash and crude oil were processed at a distance from the city's Inner Harbour, various civic officials sought a new role for the Saint John waterfront in the 1980s, soon after the Market Square development had breathed new life into the city's uptown core (Schuyler and Ircha 1987). In many ways, the visions first entertained by these earlier civic boosters foreshadowed the present conflicts between the Port's traditional client base and civic actors. The Port of Saint John's 1989 *Corporate Land Use Management Plan* highlights some of the tensions between the working port and a vibrant uptown:

> Urban waterfront property is in essence a non-renewable resource and few cities can afford to ignore the varied opportunities offered by a productive waterfront. From the perspective of both the public and private sectors, alternate land uses such as parks, marinas, residential condominiums, office towers, hotels, and tourist attractions all seem to represent natural potential developments for urban waterfronts. Port administrators, on the other hand, generally regard waterfront property as that which should be dedicated to and reserved for the traditional port functions ... It is essential that ports include land use planning in their corporate planning process in order to identify areas of potential conflict or constraint along the waterfront, to determine the optimal port-related land use for waterfront property

within the port limits, and to develop strategies to accommodate land use conflicts. (Saint John Port Corporation 1989, i)

The Port's *Corporate Land Use Management Plan* further suggested two important concepts for the future development of the waterfront. First, Pugsley Terminal, centrally located on the eastern edge of the inner harbour, was noted as the "the most suitable location [for cruise vessel activity] from the waterside and the landside." Second, Long Wharf, which is within view of the Market Square development and is the land-side asset at the furthest reach of the inner harbour, should be "perceived as a candidate for a number of alternative uses ... [that could] possibly even remove Long Wharf in its entirety from the working port" (Saint John Port Corporation 1989, 13–15). While the study obviously promoted a vibrant working port, it also envisioned a future where other land uses could potentially transform Saint John's inner harbour. The 1989 document proved to be prophetic in a number of ways. The new cruise ship terminal, opened in 2009, was built at roughly the same location as the study originally proposed. The other key site, Long Wharf, was the focus of a dramatic real estate proposal briefly entertained by Irving Oil, in 2008. The company sought to build their world headquarters on the site, and entered into a fairly complicated land swap agreement with the City of Saint John (which owned the former Lantic Sugar property, on the outer edge of the harbour) and the Port Authority to begin the development of Long Wharf. While the arrangement was welcomed by members of the Uptown Saint John Central Business District, it was strongly opposed by the local union of longshoremen (*Telegraph Journal* 2009a). In 2010, citing the worldwide recession as a reason, Irving Oil quietly abandoned their $40 million headquarters project (*Daily Gleaner* 2010).

While the 1989 *Corporate Land Use Management Plan* only alluded to land use pressures surrounding the traditional port, a much more detailed community study released over a decade later was explicit in its vision of a vastly more accessible inner harbour. The 2003 *Inner Harbour Land Use Plan*, commissioned by the Saint John Waterfront Development Partnership, called for a pedestrian-friendly, multi-use inner harbour that would ultimately transform the city and "surrounding urban region" (Urban Strategies 2003). While the plan highlighted a continued role for a "working port," and was developed in consultation with the Saint

John Port Authority, traditional port activities and related harbour fencing maintained for security reasons were not celebrated in the schematic designs. Instead, vast civic spaces, new hotels and office developments, housing, and rich cultural and heritage elements were envisioned, all linked by a series of attractive pedestrian paths. The Saint John Waterfront Development Partnership actually began construction of the first phase of a pedestrian pathway in advance of the *Inner Harbour Land Use Plan*, as the "Harbour Passage" walking and biking trail wound its way from Market Square towards the city's Harbour Bridge. The choice of the pedestrian path as an initial project was no accident, as it was meant to whet the public's appetite for a transformed inner harbour. A sympathetic 2003 editorial in the Saint John *Telegraph Journal* (2003) exclaimed: "you have to experience Harbour Passage to understand the vision and potential for the [city's] future."

While potential developments surrounding Long Wharf would ultimately be the subject of extensive press coverage in recent years (in part because the same corporate interests were both reporting on, and proposing development plans for, the Long Wharf site), other land holdings on Saint John's waterfront have also been a source of conflicting visions, if not development headaches. The Saint John Coast Guard site, strategically located adjacent to the Market Square development, has been the subject of frenzied redevelopment speculation since 2003; yet to date, redevelopment remains stalled. An early vision for a waterfront post-secondary education centre at the Coast Guard site never gained traction, and a city call for development proposals resulted in the awarding of a development contract in 2005 to the Halifax-based Hardman Group (*Telegraph Journal* 2005). Despite press reports suggesting that construction would start by 2008 at the latest, continued federal negotiations, turbulent financing conditions, and concerns over the structural soundness of some of the pilings on the wharf have all produced delays. Through it all, civic promoters have been keen to argue that the Coast Guard redevelopment is just around the corner, and that once the funding agreements are in place it will be another vital community asset in the inner harbour (*Telegraph Journal* 2009).[5] In early 2011, it was announced that waterfront officials were *"very close"* to signing a final transfer agreement with the Department of Fisheries, which still possessed the site eight years after real estate plans were first announced (*Telegraph Journal* 2011).

Beyond the optimistic press reports and schematics for hotel and condo development, the still-unrealized development of the Coast Guard site serves as a reminder of a critical role that the federal government plays in the development of port lands in Canada. In the rush to develop the federal coast guard site, civic boosters may have been too hasty in preparing for Ottawa's divestiture of the land and buildings, and may have underestimated the need for a request for continued federal involvement to help facilitate the site's transformation. As part of a civic delegation to Ottawa, one official remembered the disbelief from a federal cabinet minister when she was told that Saint John officials were placing no strings on the proposed declaration of the Coast Guard site as surplus, and simply wanted the land. According to this official, she said: "Let me get this clear, by you simply wanting the deed to the property, that would let us, the federal government, off the hook. You should want us to keep involved in some way for a long time" (Interview 7). In retrospect, this was sound advice, given that the resources of the federal treasury are much larger than those of any Canadian municipality.

FEDERAL TRANSPORTATION FACILITY DEVOLUTION: FREDERICTON INTERNATIONAL AIRPORT AUTHORITY[6]

During the federal government's dramatic deficit-cutting period in the 1990s, Transport Canada was tasked with devolving the country's airports to local authorities and others. This devolution first began in 1992 with the transfer of four of Canada's major airports – Vancouver, Edmonton, Calgary, and Montreal – to designated airport authorities. Toronto's Pearson Airport followed in 1996. In 1994, the federal government revised its National Airport Policy to transfer Canada's other major airports to designated local non-profit authorities. The resulting National Airports System (NAS) includes twenty-six major airports with significant passenger throughput volumes (200,000+), and those facilities serving provincial and territorial capitals.

The three major airports in New Brunswick (Fredericton, Saint John, and Moncton) were all within the lower margins of the required 200,000-passenger volume criterion, and each was designated part of the National Airport System. However, there was no guaranteed service level to be provided at these airports. There were rumors that Transport Canada would continue to decrease their hours of service as costs rose and revenue dropped. Transferring these Transport Canada facilities to local airport authorities enabled them to act more entrepreneurially in seeking added revenues and decreasing their operating costs. This transfer of lands and assets required intensive negotiation between the airport authorities' newly appointed boards of directors and Transport Canada.

The airport authority boards of directors were comprised of local individuals nominated by designated groups, with the initial appointments being made by the minister of Transport, on the recommendations received from the nominators. In the case of the Greater Fredericton Airport Authority (GFAA), now known as the Fredericton International Airport Authority (FIAA), the nominators to the board include the federal government (two appointees), provincial government (one), City of Fredericton (two), Town of Oromocto (one), Fredericton Chamber of Commerce (one), Enterprise Fredericton (one), and Greater Fredericton Airport Authority Board (three). Essentially, the negotiated airport transfer involved a sixty-year lease of the Fredericton airport's federal lands and chattels to a non-profit corporation. The FIAA's vision is to "provide access to the world for our people, our businesses, our institutions and our military and is a threshold to our community for visitors from the rest of the world … Our aim is to be the best small airport in the world with a facility and with people that consistently exceed the expectations of our customers and our community" (Fredericton International Airport Authority 2009).

In Moncton, negotiations were concluded swiftly, enabling the Greater Moncton Airport Authority (GMAA) to quickly accept the airport transfer and become one of the first facilities established under the new federal airports policy. However, such rapid negotiations were not without challenges. In a subsequent analysis by the federal Auditor General, Transport Canada was criticized for unfairly negotiating the initial agreement with the GMAA (Auditor General 2000). In this case, Transport Canada was found to have taken advantage of Moncton's willingness to proceed without appropriate due diligence by its directors. They had likely assumed a partnership with the federal negotiators, rather than seeking to protect the interests of the Moncton airport. Negotiations were expected to be fair between the parties, but in the initial round of discussions, seasoned federal negotiators tended to overwhelm newly minted directors.

Negotiations between the GFAA Board and Transport Canada proceeded far more cautiously and slowly. To begin with, the City of Fredericton was asked in the summer of 1997 to nominate two members to the initial GFAA Board of Directors. The mayor and council opposed the devolution of the Fredericton Airport to a local authority. This opposition was based on their perception that the federal government was downloading further responsibilities to municipalities. The city sought legal advice on the nature of their two nominations. Their concern was that although they nominated two directors, the nominees did not have a direct reporting relationship with city council. Directors were expected to exercise their fiduciary responsibility to the GFAA and were mandated to report to the city (and other nominators and stakeholders) on an annual basis. In the end, the council did nominate two directors to the GFAA Board and the initial Board took office in early 1998.

Prior to transferring the Fredericton Airport lands and chattels to the GFAA, the Board had to negotiate with Transport Canada to finalize the specific terms of the sixty-year lease. In the Fredericton case, Transport Canada's earlier capital development plans for the Fredericton Airport had included terminal upgrades and constructing an extended runway from 6,000 to 7,800 feet to serve the world's largest commercial aircraft. Prior to the federal government's mid-1990s privatization initiatives, Transport Canada had extended runways and upgraded passenger terminals in Saint John and Moncton. But the Fredericton Airport had not been dealt with. Transport Canada's subsequent transfer proposal to the GFAA was based on an "as is – where is" offer. Fredericton faced a classic "musical chairs" situation. Since the airport had not had its terminal upgraded or its runway extended prior to the new devolution policy, these capital projects were not included in Transport Canada's offer to the GFAA.

The GFAA Board was incensed over Transport Canada's intransigence on the runway issue. The Fredericton Airport was experiencing considerable difficulties in serving regional jets using the facility. The GFAA Board concluded that it would only accept the transfer of the Fredericton Airport from Transport Canada if funds were provided to extend the runway to 8,000 feet in length.

Early in the negotiations, the GFAA Board prepared an outline of principles to guide the discussions. Transport Canada officials quickly accepted the GFAA negotiating principles and signed off on them. A key principle was that negotiations would be confidential, with no public statements being made without the acknowledgment and approval of both parties. This key principle was soon violated as the federal minister of Transport, David Collenette, stood in the House of Commons and stated that under no circumstances would the Fredericton Airport receive funding for an extended runway. The minister's statement was reported by national and local media, effectively undermining much of the progress that had been achieved in the negotiations.

As discussed earlier, the City of Fredericton initially opposed the federal government's airport transfer process. The council's apparent lack of interest in the airport transfer created difficulties for the board. The negotiations appeared to have a low and, at times, negative profile within the community. To address the city's concerns and gain support from business and other regional community leaders, the board organized a one-day facilitated workshop for about two hundred major stakeholders. Key Transport Canada officials were invited to present the commercial benefits accruing to the community in having access to a major airport. Breakout groups tackled various concerns about the airport and the transfer negotiations. This workshop, entitled "This Is Your Airport," was a key milestone for the board in the negotiation process. Had the assembled Greater Fredericton community said, "walk away," the board would have resigned and left the airport in Transport Canada's hands. However, by the afternoon, it was apparent that the workshop was successful, as more and more councillors and community leaders spoke in favour of moving forward with the negotiations. It marked the turning point in the community's acceptance of the Fredericton Airport as "their facility." Many of the community's leaders came to the realization that the airport was an essential element of the region's economic infrastructure. They understood that the projected decline in service levels at the Fredericton Airport, which could occur under Transport Canada management, could lead to economic stagnation and long-term community decline. City council and the business community soon vigorously backed the board's negotiations to transfer the airport to the GFAA.

The key issue in this federal land transfer process was local community support. Without this support, it was apparent that the GFAA Board acting on its own would not have been able to continue the negotiations with Transport Canada in a meaningful manner.

The transfer negotiations continued for several years, as the main stumbling block was Transport Canada's continued refusal to fund a runway extension in the transfer agreement. In part, Transport Canada's reticence came from Minister Collenette's House of Commons statement. Essentially he had set a firm policy for federal negotiators. The GFAA Board was indifferent about how the funding was to be arranged, only that the airport should have an extended runway. The Board had many meetings with city council, members of the Provincial Legislative Assembly (MLAs), and the Honorable Andy Scott, member of Parliament and cabinet minister, seeking a solution to this difficult funding issue.

At one point, overtures were made to the military for direct support for an extended runway, as Canada's primary armed forces training establishment, CFB Gagetown, is located close to the Fredericton airport. The military would be a major beneficiary of an extended runway, as it would mean that their transport troop movements and overseas deployments could take place at Fredericton rather than at the more distant Moncton airport. However, even though the military offered considerable moral support, including assigning a senior officer to serve as liaison with the GFAA Board, they were unable to secure any funding or participate in lobbying for funds. The GFAA Board then looked to Fredericton, Oromocto, and other area municipalities for support.

These municipalities responded positively by becoming directly involved in supporting and funding the runway project, offering up their one-third share of funding support in the Infrastructure Canada Program. Not only did these area municipalities provide direct funding, they gave up their ability to support other infrastructure projects within their own communities to assist the GFAA. Infrastructure Canada agreed to contribute its one-third share, and all that remained was for the province to come forward with financial support. There was considerable stalling by the province, as they had concerns about providing infrastructure support funds to the Fredericton Airport and not to the other provincial airports.

The GFAA negotiating team held a meeting to finalize the infrastructure funding with City Councillor Walter Brown and the Honorable Brad Green, provincial Justice minister and Fredericton MLA. The negotiating team gave Brown and Green a twenty-four-hour deadline to come to an agreement with the province to support the runway extension from the Canada Infrastructure Program, or the GFAA Board would resign *en masse* with a public explanation of the many difficulties the negotiating team had encountered. A press conference was scheduled for the following afternoon. The board chair was prepared either to announce that a deal on the runway extension had been reached with the province or to announce the board members' resignations.

A hastily convened board meeting was held minutes before the press conference, and the negotiating team indicated that Minister Green had achieved a commitment from Premier Lord that the province would provide their share of the funds necessary for the runway extension. The resultant press conference was a success, with the board announcing that it was now prepared to finalize the necessary transfer arrangements with Transport Canada for the Fredericton Airport.

On 4 May 2001, the Fredericton Airport was officially transferred from Transport Canada to the Greater Fredericton Airport Authority Inc. (now the Fredericton International Airport Authority).

Although the GFAA Board faced many challenges following the transfer, the key factor in its success was the City of Fredericton's major leadership role in convincing other area municipalities, the federal government, and the province to fund the airport's runway extension. This municipal commitment to the Fredericton International Airport emerged from the community's belief that having a successful airport was vital to the continued economic and social health of Fredericton, Oromocto, and the many other communities in the upper St John River Valley. It is apparent in this case that local political leadership and support is essential for successful federal-municipal relations in dealing with federal property transfers.

The Fredericton International Airport continues to flourish. The runway was extended to 8,010 feet, the terminal building upgraded, and an international passenger arrivals area added. New international flights are arriving, military flights have increased, and overall passenger volumes continue to climb. But such success could not have come from the GFAA Board acting on its own. Municipal, provincial, and community commitment and support were crucial to the successful development of this significant federal regional transportation facility.

CONCLUSION

In New Brunswick, a small province without a dominant metropolis or history of sustained low unemployment, the issue of federal lands (and the jobs that come with them) continues to be a pressing concern for municipalities in every corner of the province. In most instances, the major New Brunswick concern is economic, reflected in job losses or gains as federal lands and activities are either diminished or expanded. As both the case studies in Miramichi and Moncton indicate, controversy emerges as the community is initially concerned about job and economic losses and struggles to retain the facility. When final abandonment decisions are made, community interests tend to shift to the federal land's potential reuse and perceived benefits to the municipality, region, and province.

In some instances, as in Moncton where the Canada Lands Company played a strong supporting role, the transition of federal lands to new use goes very well. In others, competing interests (as is the case in some Saint John port lands) or site-specific challenges (such as the shorter runway at the Fredericton airport) delay a successful transition. Broader economic forces can also undermine the successful transfer of federal land: the prolonged forestry downturn has certainly limited the prospects of Sky Park Miramichi, and the most recent severe North American recession caused Irving Oil to abandon their plans for a new headquarters on federally owned port lands in Saint John.

In the New Brunswick context, the key players in making things happen with respect to issues related to federal land are politicians, at all three government levels. Success appears to be dependent on specific political champions who can clearly and forcefully articulate the community's vision on reuse to federal officials. Having a high-ranking politician involved certainly helped move specific files forward; Premier Frank McKenna showed a specific interest in the establishment of Sky Park Miramichi, while both Fredericton and Moncton representatives enjoyed direct access to federal cabinet ministers who were able to help their home communities whenever specific problems arose (Andy Scott and Claudette Bradshaw, respectively). When a high-ranking politician is not closely attached to a specific land file, the New Brunswick experience suggests that delays are inevitable.

A second key ingredient for success is collaboration and cooperation within the community, generating commitment, vision, and support for the planned reuse of federal lands. Much of the push for renewal of the federally owned port lands within Saint John, for instance, has come from civic and business actors within the Port City who saw the long-term economic potential of the inner harbour, and started to develop and circulate detailed reports translating that potential into something concrete. While the full realization of that potential has yet to be achieved, the momentum is still there, and both federal officials and private-sector developers are cognizant of a changing waterfront. Similarly, support from the business community and surrounding municipalities was crucial in the transfer and subsequent development of the Fredericton International Airport.

Federal land acquisition and disposal is a challenging proposition in New Brunswick, and likely throughout the Maritimes. Dealing with federal lands is fraught with political and community concerns, which tend to be voiced publicly in the media and other outlets. When professional support, in the form of the Canada Lands Company, is available to help facilitate the process of transfer, the evidence suggests that it makes for an easier community transition. With provincial and municipal governments burdened with large health care, education, and infrastructure budgets, dedicating specific resources to questions surrounding surplus federal land can be a challenge – a fact that was recognized by a number of the local participants involved with the New Brunswick case studies. The federal government needs to be cognizant of these challenges, and recognize that the resources to adequately prepare for the orderly transition of federal lands are more often found in Ottawa than in the cities or towns of New Brunswick. Ensuring that federal supports for land transfer (using an agency such as the Canada Lands Company) are readily available would help ensure that New Brunswick's federal lands provide economic opportunity long after the federal jobs have left the community, and the land itself finds a compelling new use.

NOTES

1　While he was mayor, Rupert Bernard kept the letter with Prime Minister Mulroney's pledge in his wallet. He would show the letter to any National Defence official who sought to close CFB Chatham.

2　New urbanism refers to an approach in urban planning that emerged in the 1980s that advocates for "the development of compact neighbourhoods, with community facilities, stores and transit within walking distance." Some of the best known examples of "new urbanism" design include Kentlands in Maryland, Seaside in Florida, Celebration in Florida, and MacKenzie in Alberta (Leo 2002, 217). See also Jamieson et al. 2000, 467–72.

3 T.W. Acheson (1985) notes that by the mid–nineteenth century Saint John was "the third largest urban centre in British North America and the largest on its Atlantic Seaboard" (Acheson 1985, 5).

4 For a more complete examination of the port's early development, see Elizabeth McGahan. 1982. The Port of Saint John: From Confederation to Nationalization, 1867–1927. Saint John: National Harbours Board.

5 Detailed plans for the Coast Guard site's revitalization can be found at http://www.hardmangroup.ca/development/dev_coastguard.html.

6 Michael Ircha provided this section. It is based on his experience as a Fredericton-nominated director on the Board of the Greater Fredericton Airport Authority from 1998 to 2007.

INTERVIEWS

1 Captain Al Soppit, Port of Saint John. Saint John, 17 April 2009.
2 Brian Murphy, member of Parliament. Moncton, 14 January 2009.
3 Canada Lands Company Representative. Moncton, 14 January 2009.
4 Mayor of Saint John Ivan Court. Saint John, 15 March 2009.
5 Ross Jefferson, Saint John Waterfront Development. 18 March 2008.
6 Mayor of Chatham Rupert Bernard. Miramichi, 6 January 2009.
7 Steve Carson, Enterprise Saint John. Saint John, 12 March 2009.

REFERENCES

Acheson, Thomas W. 1985. *Saint John: The Making of a Colonial Urban Community.* Toronto: University of Toronto Press.

Auditor General of Canada. 2000. "The Fairness Issue." In *Transport Canada – Airport Transfers: National Airports System.* Sec. 10.94– 10.100.

Canada Lands Company. 1999. *Summary of Corporate Plan: 1999–2000 to 2003–2004.* http://www.clcl.ca/en/pdf/summary-sommaire_1999-2004.pdf.

– 2003. "Former Moncton Shops." http://www.clc.ca/success-story/former-moncton-shops.

Daily Gleaner. 2010. "Irving Oil Parent Company Cancels Office Building." 3 February.

Dion, Stéphane, Brian Slack, and Claude Comtois. 2002. "Ports and Airport Divestiture in Canada: A Comparative Analysis." *Journal of Transport Geography* 10, no. 3: 187–93.

Enterprise Miramichi. 2007. *Opportunities and Realities in the Miramichi Region: A Self Sufficiency Task Force Brief.* 28 March.

Evening Times Globe. 1982. "$70.5 Million Outlay Seen by Hatfield." 28 September.

Fredericton International Airport Authority (FIAA). 2009. *Strategic Plan: 2009–2014.* Fredericton NB.

Forbes, Ernest R. 1977. "Misguided Symmetry: The Destruction of Regional Transportation Policy for the Maritimes." In *Canada and the Burden of Unity,* edited by David J. Bercuson, 60–86. Toronto: MacMillan of Canada.

Ircha, Michael C. 1999. "Port Reform: International Perspectives and the Canadian Model." *Canadian Public Administration* 42, no. 1: 108–32.

– 2002. "Port Privatization: Commerce and Recreation." Paper presented to the 2002 Meeting of the International Association of Maritime Economists. Panama City. 13–15 November.

Jamieson, Walter, Adela Cosjin, and Susan Friesen. 2000. "Contemporary Planning: Issues and Innovations." In *Canadian Cities in Transition: The Twenty-First Century,* 2nd ed., edited by Trudi Bunting and Pierre Filion, 462–78. Don Mills ON: Oxford University Press.

Leo, Christopher. 2002. "Urban Development: Planning Aspirations and Political Realities." In *Urban Policy Issues: Canadian Perspectives,* 2nd ed., edited by Edmund Fowler and David Siegel, 215–36. Don Mills ON: Oxford University Press.

Less, A.M. 1989. *Chatham: An Airfield History.* Fredericton: Unipress.

Maclean's Magazine. 2003. "Moncton NB, CNR Shops." 11 August. Vol. 116, no. 32. http://www.macleans.ca/science/environment/article.jsp?content=20030811_63703_63703.

McGahan, Elizabeth. 1977. "The Port of Saint John, New Brunswick, 1877–1911: Exploration of an Ecological Complex." *Urban History Review* no. 3.

– 1982. *The Port of Saint John Volume 1: From Confederation to Nationalization, 1867–1927: A Study in the Process of Integration.* Saint John NB: National Harbours Board.

Miramichi Regional Development Corporation. 1979. *The Miramichi: Industrial Profile of a River Valley.* Fredericton: Province of New Brunswick.

Miramichi Weekend. 1982. "Protest Mail Reaches 16,000." 7 May.

Moncton Times. 1981. "Front Street Businesses: They'll Suffer." 5 December.

Moncton Times Transcript. 1986. "Will Gov't Influence CN's Decision on the Shops?" 17 June.

Nader, George. 1976. *Cities of Canada: Profiles of Fifteen Metropolitan Centres.* Vol. 2. Toronto: MacMillan of Canada.

NB Economic Advisor. 1973. "Government Employment in the Province of New Brunswick, 1961–71." Fredericton.

NB Economic Development, Tourism and Culture. 1999. "Three Companies to Create Jobs at Sky Park Miramichi." Fredericton. 11 January.

NB *Hansard.* 1994. New Brunswick. 23 February.

NB Municipal Affairs. 1994. *Miramichi City: Our Future Strength through Unity.* Fredericton.

Northumberland News. 1981. "Lamontagne Stuns Miramichi." 10 November.

New York Times. 1994. "The Moncton Miracle." 17 July.

Saint John. 2009. "Report to Common Council." Council meeting 2009-02-16, item 9.2(a).

Saint John Port Authority, 1978. *Port News.*

– 2009. *Annual Report 2008.*

Saint John Port Corporation. 1989. *Draft Corporate Land Use Management Plan.*

Savoie, Donald J. 2006. *Visiting Grandchildren: Economic Development in the Maritimes.* Toronto: University of Toronto Press.

Schuyler, George, and Michael C. Ircha. 1987. "Market Square: Downtown Economic Revival." *Plan Canada* 27, no. 1: 16–22.

Sky Park Miramichi. 1996. *Final Report to the Atlantic Canada Opportunities Agency.* Miramichi NB.

– 1998. *Sky Park Miramichi: An Unqualified Success.* Miramichi NB.

Statistics Canada. 2006. Census of Canada. "Population and Dwelling Counts, for Canada, Provinces and Territories, 2006 and 2001 Censuses – 100% Data."

– 2009. CANSIM Table 183-0002. "Public Sector Employment, Wages and Salaries, Seasonally Unadjusted and Adjusted, Monthly."

Telegraph Journal. 2003. "$1.95 Million Harbour Trail Opens." 27 June.

– 2005. "Project to Be Advanced in Spring." 10 January.

– 2009. "Diamond in the Rough." 29 August.

– 2009a. "Long Wharf Deal Gets Nod." 29 September.

– 2011. "Coast Guard Site Deal About to Close." 31 January.

Transport Safety Board of Canada. 1997. *Final Report of the Loss of Control on Go-around at Fredericton, New Brunswick, of an Air Canada Canadair Regional Jet, c-fski.* TBS #A 12/99, A97H0011, 16 December.

Treasury Board of Canada. 2009. *Guide to the Management of Real Property*. http://www.tbs-sct.gc.ca/rpm-gbi/doc/gmrp-ggbi/gmrp-ggbi-07-eng. aspx#a6.2.
– 2010. "Directory of Federal Real Property." http://www.tbs-sct.gc.ca/ dfrp-rbif/query_question/summary-sommaire-eng.aspx?qid=319919.
Urban Strategies. 2003. *Saint John Inner Harbour Land Use Plan*. http:// www.sjwaterfront.com/vision/inner_harbour_land_use_plan.html.
Wallace, Iain. 1975. "Containerization at Canadian Ports." *Annals of the Association of American Geographers* 65, no. 3: 433–48.
Wynn, Graeme. 1981. *Timber Colony: A Historical Geography of Early Nineteenth Century New Brunswick*. Toronto: University of Toronto Press.

4

Federal Property in Newfoundland and Labrador

STEPHEN TOMBLIN, WADE LOCKE, AND
JEFF BRAUN-JACKSON

Good governance involves working to bring different interests together, to form common perceptions, build policy communities or networks, debate issues, and facilitate the adoption of innovative practices. Conversely, finding ways to avoid narrow, parochial forms of political decision-making has never been easy in complex, autonomous, and decentralized systems of multilevel governance.

Public policy was originally designed to replace, or at least balance, old and counterproductive political forms of decision-making. Public policy was created deliberately in an era of technological-functional change to bring about improvements in functional leadership, and to generate new state-society linkages, conditions, and governance mechanisms associated with policy innovation and enhanced outcomes. Much of this has already been explored in the policy literature on Canadian federalism, albeit focused primarily on federal-provincial relations. This study, on the other hand, adopts the perspective that there are valuable lessons about federalism that can be learned from the difficulties of federal property management and from property disposition in the Newfoundland and Labrador (NL) context. NL is a jurisdiction in which the marked differences between rural and urban communities have accentuated a number of historical policy challenges (Freshwater and Tomblin 2009).

The purpose of this chapter is to explore the recent history of federal property management in Newfoundland and Labrador. Effective multilevel governance requires accountability, creating opportunities to bring divergent interests together in ways that encourage collaboration, consensus, and better implementation of ideas and policies. The case studies reviewed here clearly show that decisions about federal property management took place outside of established formal mechanisms. There was little in the way of accountability and transparency in the decisions made. Federal property management was not on the provincial media radar screen. Little in the way of criticism was reported to citizens about the decisions made with respect to federal property in the province. Many of the stakeholders interviewed expressed their concern that the process was not open and that dealing with federal officials required a tremendous expenditure of resources. Moreover, when we visited the different regions of Newfoundland and Labrador, we found that the federal government was usually working behind the scenes and offering competing projects to municipalities in order to use them as allies in fighting against the provincial government. Our case studies show, too, that federal decisions were made in isolation, with little input from municipal and provincial officials.

WORLD OF ITS OWN: PERCEPTIONS AND REALITIES CONFRONTED

NL is a province that has not witnessed much legislative reform, nor does it have a strong historical tradition of building and strengthening essential modern civil society institutions (Almond and Verba 1965; Conrad 1988; Ommer and Sinclair 2006; Sinclair 1988; Alexander 1983; Blake 1994; Hillier and Neary 1980). These circumstances have made it especially difficult to work across policy silos and generate constructive solutions to problems, not only with respect to federal property management but also in such areas as health care, education, municipal governance, and economic development.

When NL joined Canada in 1949, several formal institutions were started anew or recreated in an effort to quickly make the province more industrial and modern. For example, the municipal system of government was not well advanced, and provincial subsidies and programs helped expand the program thereafter. There was not even a pan-provincial highway system necessary to create a more integrated provincial economy. In 1949, NL lacked critical policy capacity, market capitalist, and democratic traditions. The province did not have the kind of civil society, organizations, networks, or systems of integrated communication normally associated with modern societies. Moreover, for much of its history, NL has been deeply divided internally by economic and religious cleavages, and there are embedded competing expectations and political experiences that have made it very difficult to renew governance and then reach a consensus on key technical-political issues (Freshwater and Tomblin 2009). From 1949 to 1972, Joey Smallwood took full advantage of these historical divisions to impose a policy of modernization that pitted urban against rural communities. These conditions helped mobilize a more independent, province-centred vision under the Progressive Conservative party that was led first by Frank Moores and then by Brian Peckford. In recent years this stance, fuelled by oil revenues, was reinforced by Premier Danny Williams.

In fact, the combination of powerful leaders and this sense of isolation has reinforced a focus on the need for provincial self-reliance and territorial self-determination as opposed to the adoption of common approaches to policy based on the experiences of other jurisdictions. Several of our informants suggested that NL has its own unique brand of province-building and suspicion of top-down, urban-biased, universal calls for transformation. NL is a place where there is much public cynicism about outside experts, and where it is not easy for bureaucratic or political elites to launch new ideas, frame questions, build coalition support, or gain citizen trust. Politics tend to be highly decentralized (Tomblin and Braun-Jackson 2009). In such a context, it is no surprise that picking common external enemies has proven to be a popular political strategy designed to unite the province.

Our chapter illustrates the lack of provincial involvement and commitment to securing and controlling federal property. Our informants repeatedly noted that it was sometimes difficult to get provincial politicians and bureaucrats on side to support municipal efforts in securing access to federal property. Disagreements over jurisdictional responsibilities for environmental remediation, maintenance of roads, and construction of infrastructure continue to plague relationships between provincial and federal actors.

The province's political culture has significantly affected the development of municipal government. Historically, there has not been a strong tradition of local government. In fact, British authorities in the seventeenth century forbade permanent settlement on the island. Thereafter, the development of municipal government was very slow, even in the capital, St John's, and even after Confederation

(Feehan et al. 2006). The lack of a healthy municipal governance system in the province is best summed up by the conclusion advanced in the Amulree Royal Commission report on the fiscal viability of the Dominion of Newfoundland in 1933:

> But the absence of any form of municipal government and the conduct of the entire administration of the country from St. John's, which is itself to a large extent out of touch with the outports, have had an unfortunate effect upon the people in retarding the development of a public spirit and a sense of civic responsibility ... The formation of municipal governments in the more important outports, under proper control and with the proper safeguards, would do much to induce a sense of responsibility in those called upon to contribute towards the expenses of such governments. (Feehan et al. 2009, 474–5)

Historically, few citizens have had the opportunity to participate in either municipal governance or administration. This has meant that few people are trained and qualified to act on behalf of the communities they represent. Municipal governments are weak, even within the province. Indeed, the key link between the interests of local residents and the provincial bureaucracy in St John's tends to be the local member of the House of Assembly (MHA). The MHA is expected by constituents to bring local matters to the attention of provincial decision-makers, whether it is to keep a hospital or school from closing or to expand the local highway. Municipal institutions, although improved from the time of Confederation, still show signs of weakness. Support staff in municipalities are limited, councillors tend to be poorly educated and badly paid and to work few hours, and there is generally little interest in municipal politics among the citizenry (Feehan et al. 2009).

Our respondents often noted these weaknesses when discussing the relationships between their municipalities and federal bureaucrats. In particular, local officials do not have the resources necessary to act in the best interests of their taxpayers.

OVERVIEW OF FEDERAL PROPERTY MANAGEMENT IN NEWFOUNDLAND AND LABRADOR

Our case studies demonstrate that there is a lack of coordination and joint planning among the three levels of government when it comes to federal property management in the province. One key explanation identified by political scientists is the federal government's movement away from picking "winners and losers" and instead using its fiscal capacity to assist cities and urban areas to develop their needs and economic potential. Christopher Dunn refers to this phenomenon as urban asymmetry (Dunn 2006). Dunn goes on to argue that there are mediated and non-mediated sectors with respect to community economic development, according to the intensity of provincial involvement in federal policies affecting regions and municipalities. Dunn concludes: "In the context of localism and regionalism, provincial mediation follows a logical road. There is a mediated sector and a non-mediated sector in local government matters and in community economic development matters. The province tends to involve itself – or sometimes tries to mediate – in intergovernmental relations that touch on matters affecting regional equality" (Dunn 2006, 309).

Dunn's analysis reflects the views of those persons interviewed for the study. The federal government has operated in its own orbit, it has done so behind the scenes, and it often does so without a clear guide or path to follow with respect to property management. Municipal officials are left feeling frustrated and powerless to influence the decision-making process when there is little in the way of transparency and accountability. The provincial government's involvement varies according to the region, the issue, the political stakes, and the province's finances.

THE CASES: PLACENTIA, ARGENTIA, AND HAPPY VALLEY–GOOSE BAY

The towns of Placentia, Argentia, and Happy Valley–Goose Bay provide good representative examples of the issues surrounding federal property management in the province. Placentia, on the southwest coast of the Avalon Peninsula, is home to several federal properties including the Marine Atlantic terminal at Argentia, the federal wharves in Jerseyside, and the Castle Hill National Park. Happy Valley–Goose Bay, located in central Labrador, is home to the Department of National Defence 5 Wing Goose Bay airport and base facilities, housing a combat support squadron and training facilities for the Canadian Forces and allies. This section of the chapter will review the broader issues confronting municipalities with respect to federal property management in Newfoundland and Labrador.

What are the basic issues concerning federal property management policy in the province? First, international events and pressures matter. These are far beyond the control of the province, let alone municipalities. It was the Americans, for example, who decided to abandon their base at Argentia in 1994. Similarly, the demands of the post-2001 War on Terror shaped the future of 5 Wing Goose Bay.

Second, there are unequal power relations between the federal government and local governments in the province. The DND makes decisions on the future of 5 Wing Goose Bay without any input from the town of Happy Valley–Goose Bay. But municipal governments in NL lack the capacity to mount effective lobbying campaigns to make their interests known to federal decision-makers. In Placentia, the mayor essentially handles the federal property file, and in Goose Bay, there is one individual who looks after the entire economic development file. Both Placentia and Happy Valley–Goose Bay lack sufficient funds even to fly officials to Ottawa to meet with key decision-makers in person. So municipalities tend to react to federal initiatives or intentions. They must undertake extensive lobbying campaigns to influence debates and decisions about federal property. Sometimes these campaigns involve working with the provincial government.

There are conflicts between the interests of the federal government and municipal governments. This is most starkly illustrated by Marine Atlantic in Placentia. Marine Atlantic is a Crown corporation that provides ferry service between Newfoundland and Nova Scotia. The federal government wants Marine Atlantic to be efficient and to streamline costs, while municipal politicians and businesspeople want it to be a better corporate citizen, with improved service and new investment.

Third, some issues involve the privatization of federal lands rather than their transfer to the province or local municipalities. Some property issues concern environmental legacies. American bases at both Argentia and Goose Bay were dumping grounds for a variety of toxic substances. When these properties were transferred, there were significant costs incurred in decontaminating the sites. No government, provincial or municipal, wants to be saddled with the liability of cleaning up a site. As well, municipalities must act strategically. For example, the Town of Happy Valley–Goose Bay would earn more tax revenue from private corporations operating on federal land than it does from the Department of National

Defence. However, the town is well aware that the base provides significant employment for its citizens and thus would not want to see the federal government shut down the base. On the other hand, the federal government sometimes lacks a strategic vision or plan for the future of its properties, and this makes it more difficult for parties to engage in negotiations. Finally, the need to consult broadly with the general public and specific groups such as Aboriginal peoples slows down the transfer process, though it does provide some degree of transparency and legitimacy.

Placentia: Marine Atlantic

Marine Atlantic provides seasonal ferry service between North Sydney, Nova Scotia, and Placentia. The key issue for the town is the lack of economic spin-offs from Marine Atlantic. One of our respondents noted that Marine Atlantic needs to do more to encourage people to "come and see us and stop and spend their money here" (Interview 3). The town has taken a proactive approach in trying to persuade Marine Atlantic to be a better corporate citizen. Local officials have used both formal and informal methods of lobbying. One respondent noted that communications between Marine Atlantic and the town have eroded over the past two decades. Marine Atlantic has defended itself against criticism from the town by noting that it is a federal entity and is not part of the province or the municipality. Marine Atlantic is not as interested in service to the Argentia route and making improvements there as it is in the year-round Port-aux-Basques route. As one respondent wryly remarked: "[W]e've always had the impression here that Marine Atlantic has treated the Argentia service as second-rate compared to the North Sydney service. The North Sydney service is an essential service because they have to provide it under the Constitution, and they've never looked at Argentia as an essential service (Interview 3)."

Besides Marine Atlantic, there are other federal properties that affect the livelihood of Placentia. Parks Canada administers Castle Hill National Park, which provides seasonal employment for approximately ten people. However, local officials note that Parks Canada does not seem at all interested in developing the Castle Hill site; rather, the town has been the driving force behind the creation and maintenance of historical sites. Another federal property of concern is the Argentia Access Road. This is the main highway that runs between Placentia and the Trans-Canada Highway. For years, the federal government argued that maintenance of the highway was a provincial responsibility. The province disagreed and the condition of the road gradually deteriorated over time. In 2005, the federal government finally assumed responsibility for the highway. However, the road has yet to be repaired because Ottawa wants the province to enter into a cost-sharing agreement but the province has refused to participate (Interview 2). One other issue concerning federal property management in Placentia is federal wharves. There is some evidence to suggest that the federal government wants to remove itself from maintaining the wharves. A local provincial politician understands that the federal government is "trying to get out of the business ... and they're certainly not taking on ... any more properties, and ... it's getting more and more difficult to get funding out of Small Crafts and Harbours and wharves" (Interview 2).

Placentia: The Former US Naval Base at Argentia

The American naval base at Argentia was shut down on 30 September 1994 and was taken over by the federal government. The federal government spent $106 million for the environmental remediation of the property.[1] In late 1994, the federal government announced a $5 million fund to be managed by a local development group that would be responsible for redeveloping the site. This group became the Argentia Management Authority (AMA).

From the town's perspective, the base was never a good corporate citizen. The base did not purchase materials or goods from local suppliers. The base was geographically isolated, and the Americans did their shopping on base rather than in the community. As one respondent noted, "it [the base] was not considered a part of the community, although nearly everyone in the local community worked there and everyone's lives revolved around it" (Interview 3).

Why was the property taken over by the federal government rather than the province? According to our informants, the province was uninterested because it viewed the base as being under federal jurisdiction. The costs associated with the environmental remediation were also too expensive for the province to handle. As a local official noted, "when Clyde Wells was premier [1989–95], he wrote a letter to the federal government, probably rightfully so. He said that Argentia is a federal responsibility and the province would not be participating" (Interview 1). The provincial government has not participated in the process of the transfer of the base from the federal government to the AMA. The province has not put any money into Argentia other than specific projects undertaken by the local Regional Economic Development Board.

The role of the AMA is to promote economic development in Placentia and the surrounding area. The AMA works cooperatively with both the Atlantic Canada Opportunity Agency (ACOA) and Public Works and Government Services Canada (PWGSC). The latter is primarily responsible for the environmental cleanup at the site. Of the $106 million spent on the cleanup, between seventy and eighty percent of the funding went to a Newfoundland firm. However, the AMA's strategic plan is not public (Interview 1) and there has not been any formal evaluation of the property transfer.

The province has had little involvement in Argentia. As Respondent 3 noted, the province has not "put any money into Argentia, other than specific projects that they've partnered with, which is standard all over the island" (Interview 1).

The existence of the AMA has brought some major economic spin-offs for the Argentia area. For example, the AMA has contributed over $5 million to the community during the last fifteen years. It invested $350,000 in an arena. More important, it maintained all of the municipal infrastructure in the town from 1995 to January, 2007. It brought ninety-five percent of the firefighting equipment that was on the base to the municipality. The AMA also participated in the town's marketing, signage, and mapping programs, investing $600,000 in a walking trail program, and $200,000 in an RV park. Finally, the AMA is working toward establishing a museum to tell the story of Argentia (Interview 1).

But all of this is not enough to satisfy the local people. Due to amalgamation in 1993, Argentia is now part of the municipality of Placentia. But taxes are not paid on the former base as on other properties in the municipality. A local official in Placentia noted that the AMA is "paying 100,000 dollars a year – it's now about 3 percent of our budget. They should be paying a lot more" (Interview 3).

Happy Valley–Goose Bay: 5 Wing Goose Bay

The DND's 5 Wing Goose Bay is the most important federal property in the community. The bases involve 5,400 hectares of DND land

and infrastructure, and private owners use or have bought small areas of land or infrastructure. The size of the base has not changed since the arrival of the Americans in early 1940, although there were transfers back and forth with Public Works and Transport Canada before the late 1980s (Interviews 7, 8, and 9). Unlike most other bases in Canada, 5 Wing Goose Bay is an active base with civilian aviation operators working from DND lands. Some land was sold in the late 1990s through pressure from Public Works Canada, against the wishes of the DND (Interviews 7, 8, and 9). So 5 Wing Goose Bay is a complex "coming together of the two very different worlds that are out there: the DND world that needs to be there for strictly DND operation, and the world of commerce and private enterprise and commercial opportunity and developing Goose Bay. There has to be a clear understanding or an overlap of those worlds" (Interview 10).

What was involved with the federal property transfer process in Goose Bay? The criteria the DND uses to determine divesture of property are based on its "operational requirements." They study requests for property on a case-by-case basis, moving up through the chain of command in the DND: "national defence headquarters has the final say" (Interviews 7, 8, and 9). If the DND wants to divest itself of property, it is first offered to other federal agencies, then to the provincial government, and finally to the municipal government. Negotiations are handled through the Treasury Board. The town of Goose Bay was given training about the federal property transfer process from a federal bureaucrat who was not identified (Interview 6).

What has the DND contributed to Goose Bay through the operation of the base? The base has been the key economic driver in the town for decades. The Department has spent millions of dollars on an annual basis, and the base employs a significant number of people in the community. The base is generous with local groups: "in a run of a year … we had something like $65,000 worth of non-military use made of our property and whatnot, of which $58,000 we waived the cost. So we're big supporters of this community" (Interviews 7, 8, and 9).

For the community, the military operations provide an important source of employment. However, the taxes paid to the town from the properties on the base are less than equivalent civilian properties would bring. The town does not receive any business taxes from DND operations, but it does from the private businesses that work

from base property (Interview 6). This issue is particularly important at Goose Bay: it "seems here there are more issues with regards
to PILT [payment in lieu of taxes] and buildings coming down than
other bases that I've been stationed at. There's always a concern in
every base and community because PILT is ... [a] revenue stream; but
here it's even more sensitive. I think that's also tied to the fact of the
question of about Goose Bay in the future" (Interviews 7, 8, and 9).
The town is not interested in owning the entire base infrastructure
due to the cost of maintenance.

Our Goose Bay respondents identified four problems with respect
to the federal property transfer process. First, there is no clear property transfer process for this case because it is unique: the base is
still active while being downsized and opened to uses by other levels
of government and private actors. The process of federal property
transfer "only seems to work for bases that are closed. There's nothing there for bases that are downsizing, and we're somewhat caught
in the middle because nothing can be done right now because we're
still waiting to see whether we're going to get promises from the
government or whether it's going to be status quo or what" (Interviews 4, 5, and 6). Moreover, "there doesn't seem [to be] clear-cut
instructions on what to do with this stuff" (Interview 6). The town
council is not sure of the process whereby private companies can get
access to base land.

5 Wing Goose Bay remains active, which tends to complicate the
typical property transfer process. As our respondents noted, in a
typical situation, a base closes and "the municipality could go in
and acquire whatever they want" but "anything that becomes vacant
here ... we have to wait until DND makes a decision on it because
it's still an active base ... [That said, we are] not promoting closure
of the base. That's the last thing ... I want to see" (Interviews 4, 5,
and 6). The town has developed a governance structure to prepare
for base closure and marketing the infrastructure. This plan was
developed through the assistance of the Harris Centre at Memorial
University of Newfoundland, which specializes in public policy and
regional development (Interview 6).

A second problem is that a significant portion of the base property
is in the hands of Canada's foreign allies. As our respondents noted,
the property belongs to DND but some of the infrastructure belongs
to other nations' militaries, and the federal government is trying to
negotiate the residual value of these properties. The transfer from

allies to DND can take up to six years (Interviews 4, 5, and 6). It is in the interest of DND to extend these negotiations as long as possible, because with each year that passes, those properties are worth less in residual value (Interview 5).

A third problem is that the Department of National Defence has had difficulty making decisions for the base, because it lacks a strategic framework. Several factors complicate decision-making about the base. First, its viability and strategic importance depend on unpredictable international events, such as the war in Afghanistan. The potential for future requirements induces much caution in planning for the base's future. As well, there are financial exigencies exacerbated by the recent recession. Finally, consultations with Aboriginal groups must be carried out when property is sold or transferred, and this can greatly slow down the decision-making process (Interviews 4, 5, and 6).

The final significant problem concerns the relationships between the town and the federal government. Of course the community's goal is to keep the base viable, and municipal officials lobby the federal government to maintain it. But from the local viewpoint the relationship with the DND is, at best, "positive with reservations" (Interviews 4, 5, and 6). Goose Bay officials perceive DND staff as very secretive, reluctant to share information. The town is highly suspicious, wondering whether the DND people that they deal with are being honest: "they'll look you in the eye and tell you one thing, and we have suspicions they're doing something else" (Interviews 4, 5, and 6). A Goose Bay official sardonically remarked that "you can't get any specifics from them – nothing is cut and dried with these people – nothing" (Interview 6).

For their part, DND officials argue that they have engaged in a fair amount of communication with municipal officials. DND representatives from the base meet with the citizens' coalition and the chamber of commerce. The DND is also a member of the Central Labrador Economic Development Board and they participate in the Goose Bay Airport Development Committee (Interviews 7, 8, and 9). Of greater significance for the base officials is the perception that the Town meddles in its affairs. DND representatives feel that they cannot make decisions to demolish buildings on the base because of the politics involved. As our respondents noted, "without demolishing unsafe buildings, you literally start to incur a bunch of liabilities … for trying to maintain buildings that literally should have been demolished" (Interviews 7, 8, and 9). DND representatives resent this political meddling in their decisions. The Department is particularly frustrated because those protesting the demolition of DND buildings do not themselves seem interested in taking over the buildings. In response to this type of protest, DND will ask the municipality or province to "give us your answer in whatever period of time it was, and it literally took us three months to get past that – just to get an indication from either the province or municipality that they were interested in it. After the three-month period, we missed an entire construction season" (Interviews 7, 8, and 9).

The bottom line for town officials is that power relations are uneven. The base exists only with the blessing of the federal government. As one official noted, if the Harper government announced tomorrow that the base would be closed, "all [the town] could do is shout and bawl, lobby and fight" (Interviews 4, 5, and 6). At the same time, the local DND representatives have little influence in decisions about federal property transfers or a potential base closure. There is no local discretion about such matters: as officials describe the situation, "I don't make policy – and none of us do. We're required, you know, to fulfill the policy and undertake it" (Interviews 7, 8, and 9).

The town's greatest fear is that the base will be closed. As one respondent noted, "the chief of defence staff has said that he has no use for Goose Bay. He doesn't see it as an asset to him with regard to any training that they require at the moment. The cost to DND to operate and maintain the base is substantial, $110,000,000 a year. It's hard to justify that cost if the base isn't being used" (Interview 6). However, the Harper government has assured the town that "they are actively seeking uses for that base." Even better, the Conservative government assured the town that "they have an operational requirement for 5 Wing Goose Bay" (Interviews 4, 5, and 6). A key problem is that the process of decision-making about the base's future is complex and is taking place far from Goose Bay. As the DND respondents noted, "the department is going to have their proposal to the minister ... and he will make that decision based on what the military is providing them, and then he has to bring it to caucus and he has to get caucus to agree to this defence strategy; and there's the Privy Council involved because this whole defence strategy needs to be affordable ... So there's, you know, Privy Council, probably Treasury Board, and then the Conservative caucus.

Now we see the Opposition are going to have their comments; but, because it's a minority government … that means you're going to have to have them onside as well. And so we're quite far down the food chain in the decision process – wearing a uniform – and then us being here in Goose [Bay], we're even further down the food chain" (Interviews 7, 8, and 9).

There have also been conflicts between the municipality and the federal government over rezoning and the water supply. The DND is frustrated by the town's decision to develop a residential area very near the base's runways, just outside the base border. As the base representatives noted, "if it [the residential development] encroaches on the ability of us to be able to take off and land aircraft, it [the base] is of no value in terms of a military operation requirement" (Interviews 7, 8, and 9). The DND contacted both the provincial Intergovernmental Affairs Ministry and the Ministry of Municipal Affairs to have them persuade the Town to amend its rezoning plans. With respect to the water supply, the base supplies Goose Bay with all of its water. The Town pays between $10,000 and $12,000 per month for the service but does not have control over the supply. The Town wants the base to increase the water pressure, but the base is reluctant to do so.

The most important transfer of federal property that has occurred in Goose Bay was that given to the Goose Bay Airport Corporation (GBAC). It took over nine years – and significant legal fees – for GBAC to lease the land, which it will have the opportunity to purchase, or continue to lease, after three years (Interviews 4, 5, and 6). GBAC is a not-for-profit, public corporation. Fifty percent of the public members of this airport authority's board are elected by their respective organizations (that is, the municipal government and the chamber of commerce), and the other fifty percent are elected at the annual general meeting. The latter members represent private businesses in the community. Revenues for GBAC come from the airport improvement fee, leases from corporate tenants, federal support from the Atlantic Canada Opportunities Agency (ACOA) to expand operations, and DND spending (for example, the resurfacing of the airport runways). Any profits are reinvested back into the corporation.

In July 2007, GBAC commenced a three-year lease of buildings and land from DND. The airport corporation then sublet both the buildings and the land to a variety of businesses, often at very generous rates, in order to spur economic growth. The tenants include:

- Provincial Aerospace
- Aurora (uranium)
- Air Labrador
- RCMP
- North Winds Aviation
- Irving
- Woodward Group
- Provincial Airlines

The property transfer negotiation process involved a great many meetings and discussions between GBAC's board of directors, the DND in Ottawa, and DND officials at the base. There were several stakeholders involved in the process, including the federal civil service (DND and Public Works), GBAC, and the community. With so many stakeholders, respondents noted, the transfer process was slow. For one thing, there was no transfer model in place to help guide this process due to the uniqueness of the case. It involved some privatization on a base that was still active (Interview 10). As well, there was a lack of continuity in the DND staff conducting the negotiations. A respondent describes this as "organizational games": "sending people to meetings for one time and then the next time it's a new person" (Interview 10). Finally, the issues at stake were many and complex. They involved the footprint to be occupied by the Airport Corporation, but also all "the servicing agreements of what would be required from each part because, obviously, the snow clearing, municipal services and garbage and everything like that that has to be taken into consideration" (Interview 10).

The municipality has been assertive in its demands with respect to the base and has lobbied the federal and provincial governments. For example, in 2007 the Town sent two letters to the newly installed defence minister (Peter MacKay) asking for meetings about the future of the base. However, no substantive response was received from the minister. Officials from municipalities that have experienced base closures have advised the town: "Don't trust anyone and you got to go sit in their face all the time. Go to Ottawa and 'camp out'" (Interviews 4, 5, and 6). Stakeholders involved in the town's lobbying efforts include the provincial government, the trade union representing the base employees, and the Goose Bay Concerned Citizens' Coalition. This last group was established in 2004 and is composed of representatives from local businesses, the chamber of commerce, municipal council, union memberships, and GBAC. However, the group has had limited interaction with representatives from the base and is more likely to advance its issues through the media rather than face-to-face (Interviews 7, 8, and 9).

The provincial government has always been supportive of the base. One respondent noted that "on election night I found it interesting in Danny Williams' speech to his party supporters and to the people of the province who were watching. I have to say I was encouraged by the only file that he did mention by name was 5 Wing Goose Bay" (Interview 4). The lead provincial actor with respect to 5 Wing Goose Bay is Intergovernmental Affairs. One respondent noted that the ministry has been fully engaged with the file and they work well with the town (Interview 6).

In 2004, municipal officials went on a "lessons learned" tour to other municipalities that had experienced base closures. They found that towns could have a successful post-closure existence if there was a collaborative effort between the municipality and the provincial and federal governments. Often their success depended on a "champion" from the federal or provincial government (Interviews 4, 5, and 6).

An important feature of the Town's lobbying efforts is the relationship between local stakeholders and federal politicians. When the Liberals were in power, the town found it easier to get its voice heard at the cabinet table and within government. The former member of Parliament for Labrador, Lawrence O'Brien, had a good working relationship with Prime Ministers Chrétien and Martin. As one respondent noted, the member "lived in Goose Bay; he worked in Goose Bay. He was personal friends with Paul Martin … And when Lawrence died, Paul Martin was here at his funeral, as well as a number of ministers came in … that was a level of commitment. People in this town knew Paul Martin on a first name basis, and … they've got a lot of contacts within the Liberal bureaucracy … Now when the government changed, that level, of course, dropped" (Interview 6). Similarly, it is easier to get the town's position heard when relationships are built with the minister of defence. However, this was weakened when Peter MacKay was appointed as minister: "up until the change of the position, minister of defence, you know, we had an open line of communication with Minister O'Connor's office and we've tried to establish that line of communication and, to date, all we've been told ... all we've received is a very short letter saying – we acknowledge receipt of your letter" (Interviews 4, 5, and 6).

CONCLUSION

Federal property management in Newfoundland and Labrador lacks clarity, focus, transparency, and accountability. As is evident from interviews with stakeholders, there is little coordination and cooperation across levels of government about the transfer of federal properties.

There are several explanations for this phenomenon. First, municipalities in Newfoundland and Labrador (with the exception of the greater St John's metropolitan area) lack the policy and fiscal capacity to act as champions for the management of federal properties. Officials do not have the resources at hand to constantly engage decision-makers in Ottawa, or to make them aware of local concerns. At times, political channels can bring pressure to bear on federal decision-makers, but this mechanism is highly personalistic, intermittent, and dependent on shifting partisan alignments.

Second, the provincial government generally plays a limited role in facilitating the management of property transfers to municipal governments. The province has not provided financial assistance or expertise to local governments to allow them to assume responsibility for former federal properties. And the provincial government is reluctant to assume financial obligations, especially when it can argue that maintenance costs and other expenses are Ottawa's responsibilities. In part this reflects ongoing disputes between the provincial and federal governments over transfer payments and control of the offshore oil and gas resources.

Third, the federal government lacks clarity of direction with respect to its inventory of property in the province. Even if local officials were in a position to assume responsibility for a property, decision-makers in Ottawa often do not have a clear plan about how to dispose of their holdings. Our respondents provided ample evidence of the frustration that this causes. Local officials are forced to respond to decisions regarding federal property management in isolation, without opportunities for feedback and input. Federal property management in Newfoundland and Labrador must be viewed through the lenses of rural-urban divisions, the lack of fiscal

and policy capacity especially at the municipal level, and the deeply
rooted mistrust of outside experts and their ideas.

NOTE

1 http://www.argentia.ca/directors.html.

INTERVIEWS

1 Official, Argentia Management Authority, Placentia.
2 Provincial politician, Placentia.
3 Municipal official, Placentia.
4 Municipal official, Happy Valley–Goose Bay.
5 Municipal official, Happy Valley–Goose Bay.
6 Municipal official, Happy Valley–Goose Bay.
7 Officer, 5 Wing Goose Bay.
8 Officer, 5 Wing Goose Bay.
9 5 Wing Goose Bay.
10 Official, Goose Bay Airport Corporation.

* Interviews 4, 5, and 6 and 7, 8, and 9 were conducted as group interviews.

REFERENCES

Alexander, David. 1983. *Atlantic and Confederation.* Toronto: University
    of Toronto Press.
Almond, Gabriel, and Sidney Verba. 1965. *The Civic Culture.* Boston:
    Little, Brown and Company.
Blake, Raymond. 1994. *Canadians at Last: Canada Integrates Newfound-
    land as a Province.* Toronto: University of Toronto Press.
Bradford, Neil. 1998. *Commissioning Ideas: Canadian National Policy
    Innovation in Comparative Perspective.* Toronto: Oxford University
    Press.
Cairns, Alan. 1988. *Constitution, Government and Society in Canada.*
    Toronto: McClelland and Stewart.
Conrad, Margaret. 1988. "The Atlantic of the 1950's." In *Beyond Anger
    and Longing: Community and Development in Atlantic Canada,* edited
    by Berkely Flemming, 55–96. Fredericton: Acadiensis.
Dunn, Christopher. 2006. "Urban Asymmetry and Provincial Mediation of
    Federal-Municipal Relations in Newfoundland and Labrador." In

Canada: The State of the Federation 2004 – Municipal-Federal-Provincial Relations in Canada, edited by Robert Young and Christopher Leuprecht, 297–331. Montreal & Kingston: McGill-Queen's University Press for the Institute of Intergovernmental Relations.

Feehan, James P., Jeffery Braun-Jackson, Ronald Penney, and Stephen G. Tomblin. 2009. "Newfoundland and Labrador." In *Foundations of Governance: Municipal Government in Canada's Provinces,* edited by Andrew Sancton and Robert Young, 453–86. Toronto: University of Toronto Press.

Freshwater, David, and Stephen G. Tomblin. 2009. "Making Sense of Changing Realties in the Uncharted Fringe." In *Remote Control: Governance Lessons for and from Small, Insular, and Remote Regions,* edited by Godfrey Baldacchino, Rob Greenwood, and Larry Felt, 19–46. St John's: Institute of Social Economic Research.

Hillier, James, and Peter Neary. 1980. *Newfoundland in the 19th and 20th Centuries.* Toronto: University of Toronto Press.

McDonald, Ian G.H., and James K. Hillier, eds. 1987. *To Each His Own: William Coaker and the Fisherman's Protective Union in Newfoundland Politics, 1908–1925.* St John's: Institute of Social Economic Research.

Ommer, Rosemary, and Peter Sinclair. 2006. *Power and Restructuring: Canada's Coastal Society and Environment.* St John's: Institute of Social Economic Research.

Pierson, Neil. 2000. "Increasing Returns, Path Dependency, and Study of Politics." *American Political Science Review* 94, no. 2: 251–63.

Pross, A. Paul. 1993. *Group Politics and Public Policy, 2nd ed.* Toronto: Oxford University Press.

Simeon, Richard. 1972. *Federal-Provincial Diplomacy.* Toronto: University of Toronto Press.

Sinclair, Peter, ed. 1988. *A Question of Survival.* St John's: Institute of Social Economic Research.

Tomblin, Stephen. 2003. "Ability to Manage Change Through Regionalization: Theory Versus Practice." Paper presented to the Australasian Political Studies Association Conference, University of Tasmania, 29 September–1 October.

– 2007. "Effecting Change and Transformation through Regionalization." *Canadian Public Administration,* Spring: 1–20.

Tomblin, Stephen, and Jeff Braun-Jackson. 2009. "Renewing Health Governance: A Case-Study of Newfoundland and Labrador." *Canadian Political Science Review* 3, no. 4: 15–30.

5

The Development of the Toronto Waterfront: Federal Presence, Institutional Complexity, and Planning Outcomes

CHRISTOPHER SANDERSON AND PIERRE FILION

INTRODUCTION

Waterfront planning in Toronto stands out from usual land use planning processes by the intermittent involvement of all levels of government and the intense public interest stemming from high expectations regarding this site. Toronto waterfront planning has been marked by repeated changes of priority, largely as a result of the presence of multiple agencies, each with its specific interests and agendas, but also as a function of its long history and the societal transitions that have occurred over time.

This chapter gives particular attention to the presence of the federal government at critical junctures in the planning of the waterfront. Since local and regional governments have the mandate for land use planning, federal involvement in it has been a source of tension. Constitutionally, the federal government is removed from the land use planning process, but its spheres of responsibility (e.g., ports and airports), its land-holdings, and its ability to fund redevelopment drew it in. Most federal interventions regarding the Toronto waterfront took place indirectly, via semi-autonomous agencies. At different times, however, the federal government felt compelled to intervene directly or to create or replace agencies to push through its policy agenda for waterfront lands. Another consequence of the federal role has been the subjugation of land use planning to other objectives. There is evidence of electoral motivations driving federal involvement, and budgetary imperatives having a key influence on waterfront interventions by the federal government and the agencies it created. Beyond its focus on the federal role, this study is also about how a complex and shifting administrative environment reflects on policy outcomes.

The chapter consists of a historical narrative of the evolution of the Toronto waterfront from the early years of the twentieth century until 2007. The account highlights the impacts of major economic transitions and of public sector interventions, linked to the transition of the waterfront from transportation (port and railway) and industrial functions, to a residential, recreational, and tourism orientation. It underscores the important roles of several agencies in waterfront planning and development: the Toronto Harbour Commission, the Harbourfront Corporation (now the Toronto Port Authority), the Canada Lands Company, and the Toronto Waterfront Revitalization Corporation (recently relabelled Waterfront Toronto). The historical narrative leads to a discussion about the importance of different factors in the evolution of Toronto waterfront planning. This discussion considers the presence of different levels of government, the creation of agencies each pursuing their own agendas, urban development tendencies, changing planning processes and urban development models, and society-wide value and economic trends.

The chapter links these factors to outcomes. Today, the waterfront is largely redeveloped, much of it occupied by high-rise buildings, with a relatively small proportion of its space given to parks and other public areas. Moreover, there are conflicting land uses along the waterfront and as yet little interconnection among its different sectors. The chapter demonstrates how these features are direct consequences of planning processes, institutional arrangements, and broader societal and economic contexts. The history of Toronto waterfront planning has been one of high expectations but far more modest outcomes, due to coordination difficulties and the secondary importance given to planning objectives in the waterfront redevelopment process.

The chapter draws from several sources of information. Documents covering decades of planning for the Toronto waterfront were supplemented by newspaper content analysis and twelve in-depth interviews. Two thousand *Globe and Mail* and *Toronto Star* articles covering a forty-year period were consulted. While newspapers are obviously not free from bias, they are well suited to reconstructing historical events, such as the protracted waterfront planning and redevelopment process, marked by repeated debates and controversies. Interviews with members of Parliament, heads of development agencies, and urban planners added to these documented information sources. Each interview was one hour long and involved semistructured questions on policy-making, intergovernmental relations, social forces, and policy evaluation.

The study centres on parts of the old City of Toronto waterfront that were, or still are, occupied by port, industrial, and railway functions and airport uses. The portion of the waterfront that is under investigation is 6.5 kilometers long and covers approximately ten square kilometers, running from Leslie Street in the east to Stratchan Avenue in the west, and includes port installations to the east, Harbourfront at the centre, and the railway lands to the west.

THE HARBOUR-INDUSTRIAL PHASE (EARLY TWENTIETH CENTURY TO THE LATE 1950S)

Toronto owes its early existence to its strategic lakeshore location. It was natural that the lake frontage would be occupied by port-related facilities. The waterfront's transportation focus was further reinforced by the location of railway facilities – main lines, marshalling yards, and maintenance installations – immediately north of the downtown portion of the port (Mellen 1974). (With the later addition of an airport and the Gardiner Expressway, all transportation modes could be found along the waterfront.) Access to different transportation modes along with a plentiful supply of land on the waterfront encouraged industrial uses, many relying on port facilities and requiring large sites.

A powerful local growth coalition led by the Toronto Board of Trade challenged the dominance of the railroad companies and lobbied for improved port facilities along with further industrial development along the waterfront (Schaeffer 1974). In response, in 1911 the federal government created the Toronto Harbour Commission (THC). The purpose of the THC was to manage and improve port facilities, as well as to attract industries on land reclaimed from Lake Ontario. It was given the power "to acquire, expropriate, hold, sell, lease and otherwise dispose of such real estate ... as it may deem necessary or desirable for the development, improvement, maintenance and protection of the harbour" (Government of Canada 1911).

Control of the waterfront was effectively ceded to the THC, which was structured as a quasi-governmental body, controlled by a board of five: three being appointees of the city, one of the governor-general-in-council, and one of the governor-general-in-council under advisement of the Toronto Board of Trade. The THC was granted ownership of most of the waterfront (about eighty percent of the land) and its land reclamation activity considerably expanded this area, adding land all along the waterfront (Toronto Harbour Commissioners 1912) (see Figure on next page).

There was little federal involvement in THC affairs until the 1980s. Of course, as the federal government had created the Commission it could technically modify its letters patent, but in practice, it was the city that oversaw the THC's finances and nominated a majority of its board members. Over the years, the THC was left out of legislation that brought other harbour agencies under federal control. It remained independent of Transport Canada and other federal administrative bodies (Ircha 1993). The main interface with federal policy concerned the THC's port function, but this was not its core activity, given its focus on industry and real estate. The lack of federal engagement is described by a former board member and general manager (Interview 1): "From the Feds this was seen as the Port of Toronto operation … There was no interference. There was no dialogue, really. The only dialogue I ever had was attending a seminar or get-together of authorities from ports throughout Canada. Certainly, there was no pressure put on us. I had no separate meetings with any representative from the government or any request that I conduct myself in a certain manner." Both the city and the federal government provided the THC with start-up funding, but it was expected to raise the bulk of its money from public debentures. The THC was to use this money to generate revenues by creating and selling or leasing industrial land. Like many harbour agencies of the time, the THC was viewed by its commissioners as a real estate operation, whose port functions often took backstage to industrial development (Merrens 1988, 96). The federal government did ratify transportation strategies adopted by the THC. The federal government, in conjunction with the City of Toronto, authorized the creation of the Toronto Island Airport in 1937 (Royal Commission on the Future of the Toronto Waterfront 1991, 377) and the piecemeal development of an outer harbour on both sides of the Leslie Spit, a complex pattern of reclaimed land jutting out 4.65 kilometers into Lake Ontario (Merrens 1988, 100). The

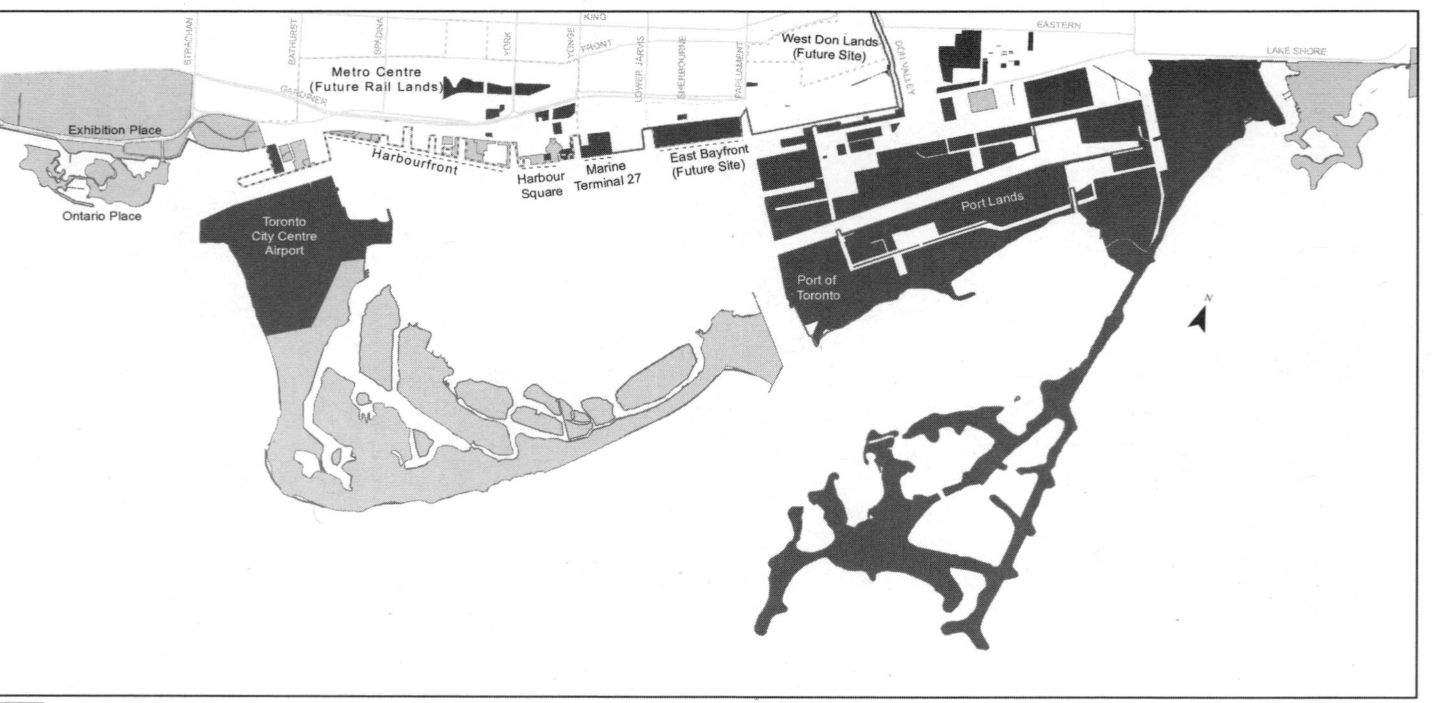

Toronto Harbour Commission Land Ownership (1980)

outer harbour was never completed, and what was built is now used for recreation and park space.

The THC's activities were limited by the modest importance of the port. Before the 1958 opening of the St Lawrence Seaway, seafaring vessels could not reach Toronto, which confined the port to inland marine traffic. High hopes were vested in the opening of the Seaway, but these were soon dashed by a much smaller increase in tonnage than anticipated. And as containerization took hold in the 1970s, the Toronto harbour was further marginalized because it was inaccessible to virtually all containerized vessels (Booz, Allen, and Hamilton 1992). Toronto could not compete in this regard with Montreal, Halifax, or Quebec (Ramlalsingh 1975, 53). The Toronto Port recorded its highest shipping throughput in 1969, which quickly decreased thereafter (Royal Commission on the Future of the Toronto Waterfront 1989a). The lack of port traffic had, by the 1970s, plunged the THC into a financial crisis, spurring it to dispose of its land to generate revenue (Royal Commission on the Future of the Toronto Waterfront 1989b, 47).

The THC's industrial development strategy did not fare much better than its port initiatives. Industry on the Commission's lands remained limited to low-value and land-hungry sectors, including concrete works, coal yards, an oil refinery, and storage (Lemon 1990, 16). Nonetheless, the industrial status of the waterfront was confirmed by the City of Toronto's first Official Plan (City of Toronto Planning Board 1950). However, the sector's industrial designation flew in the face of contemporary reality. By the end of the 1940s, these industrial functions were in serious decline and the new trend toward suburbanization caused the waterfront lands to be overlooked by new industries, practically bringing an end to waterfront land sales (Desfor 1993). Multi-storey, rail- and marine-dependent factories in the Toronto central area were abandoned for single-storey, truck-accessible plants in the suburbs (Donald 2002, 2133; Filion 2001).

Despite repeated refinancing, the financial structure of the THC obligated it to sell land and continually seek other growth opportunities to support its port-related and land-reclamation activities (Royal Commission on the Future of the Toronto Waterfront 1989b, 44).

The period from the early twentieth century until the mid-1950s is characterized by compatibility between the institutional structure – essentially the THC – and the pursuit of port- and industrial-oriented development on waterfront lands. There was little public or political interest in the waterfront beyond support for expanding port and industrial installations.

THE POST-INDUSTRIAL PHASE (FROM THE 1960S TO THE 1980S)

In this chapter the expression "post-industrial" is given two meanings: the transition from industrial to non-industrial waterfront land uses and, more generally, changes of values at a societal scale, which entail, among other things, more importance given to leisure and the consumption of services.

Early Planning for New Waterfront Land Uses

There is no clearly identifiable point of transition between the industrial and post-industrial phases. But on the waterfront, one could set the inception of the post-industrial phase as early as 1959. This marked the beginning of a City of Toronto planning process leading to a call for the replacement of waterfront port and industrial uses directly south of the downtown. Two years later, Metro Toronto engaged in a comprehensive planning exercise for the Metro-wide waterfront. Alternatively, the shift to the post-industrial phase could be signalled by the 1972 construction of the first development marking a functional shift on the waterfront: Harbour Square, a hotel-residential complex on the Lakefront between Yonge and York Streets.

For three decades, from the early 1950s to the late 1970s, urban issues assumed prominence on the federal agenda. The CMHC (Central Mortgage and Housing Corporation, since renamed Canada Mortgage and Housing Corporation) guaranteed a high proportion of the mortgages that encouraged single-family-home construction, which promoted planned suburban subdivisions to secure the long-term value of the mortgaged properties (Bacher 1993; Miron 1993). From 1954 until 1968, the federal government also funded urban renewal. In 1968, the federal government withdrew from conventional urban renewal, but maintained its involvement in urban revitalization by launching the Neighbourhood Improvement Program in 1973. Further evidence of federal interest in urban matters was provided by the 1971 creation of the Ministry of State for Urban Affairs (disbanded in 1979), whose aim was to formulate and coordinate urban-oriented federal policy with other levels of government (Wolfe 2003). It is in this context and in the aftermath of Expo 67 in Montreal and the 1971 opening of Ontario Place in Toronto (two water-oriented recreational-cultural projects) that the opportunity for federal intervention on Toronto's waterfront presented itself.

A developer and prominent Liberal, William Teron, proposed to a federal member of Parliament the idea of assembling waterfront industrial property for a park. The idea was accepted by the federal cabinet, and negotiations soon began for the purchase of under-utilized industrial waterfront sites (Gordon 1994, 6; Mclaughlin 1992, 9). The proposal for parkland was subsequently cited as a "gift" to Toronto during the 1972 electoral campaign, but electoral results were disappointing. The Liberals lost seven seats in Toronto as well as their majority status. nationally. The parkland proposal resurfaced in the mid-1970s, under the new guise of Harbourfront.

The federal government was not alone in having an interest in future waterfront uses. In the late 1950s and early 1960s, both Metro Toronto and the City of Toronto became involved in waterfront planning. Sensing mounting interest for a redevelopment of industrial and harbour lands, Metro launched what would turn out to be a protracted Metro-wide waterfront planning process. The city, meanwhile, departed from its traditional attachment to industrial functions on the waterfront, and took a position in favour of non-industrial uses on the central waterfront – the portion of the waterfront adjacent to the downtown (Desfor 1993; Desfor, Goldrick, and Merrens 1989; Goldrick and Merrens 1990; Hodge 1972; Macaulay 1992; Royal Commission on the Future of the Toronto Waterfront 1989b).

In reaction to the departure of a steamship line and the resulting need to find a new purpose for the central waterfront, city planners launched a study of the district in 1959 (Toronto Planning Board 1962). Their report rejected introducing housing on the waterfront because of the absence of neighbourhood amenities and incompatibility with remaining industrial uses (Toronto Planning Board 1962, 5). It opted instead for a highly modernist scheme, involving a series of elevated decks and plazas which would create a walkway connecting the downtown with the waterfront by bridging railway lands and the Gardiner Expressway. This would reduce the impact of these obstacles and, more generally, of distance. The report proposed a collection of low-rise institutional buildings at the water's edge.

Failed Planning Visions and Early Redevelopment Projects

The recommendations of the report were integrated into planning proposals for downtown Toronto (City of Toronto Planning Board 1963). However, while city planners were still engaged in the production of planning reports for the central waterfront, city councillors short-circuited this process by endorsing a plan for a large-scale residential and hotel development prepared by Marvo Construction Ltd, the new owner of the waterfront between Yonge and York Streets (a district labelled Harbour Square). This project had already been approved by the THC. In effect, the adoption of the Harbour Square plan by the City of Toronto and the THC ended attempts to deal with this district as part of a waterfront-wide comprehensive plan (*Globe and Mail* 1963a). Even Metro Toronto, which was at the time engaged in a planning process for the entire waterfront, endorsed the privately planned development (*Globe and Mail* 1963b). The city, the Toronto Harbour Commission, and the developer engaged in an exchange of property and leases that allowed the development to proceed (*Globe and Mail* 1965). When one of the major financial backers of the project collapsed, Campeau Corporation took over.

Campeau made design changes, contending that only "luxury and super-luxury" suites were economically feasible on the site (Dutton 1969). The Toronto Planning Board rezoned the area and city planners adapted the plans to provide some level of public access (Dutton 1969). The project was quickly approved by Toronto City Council in 1969. But because of the 1969–70 recession, work did not begin until the spring of 1972.

In 1967, Metro Toronto adopted recommendations of the comprehensive planning process that had begun in 1961 (Metropolitan Toronto Planning Board 1967). The planning process was exceptionally complex, bringing together all the agencies involved with the waterfront. However, responsibility for delivering the final plans for the city's portion of the waterfront fell to the Toronto Harbour Commission. Proposals were incorporated into a document entitled *A Bold Concept for the Redevelopment of the Toronto Waterfront* (Toronto Harbour Commission 1968). The main features of the plan were the creation of an outer harbour, the relocation of the existing airport, and the construction of a new residential community on the old airport site. The airport relocation proposal was critical to the THC because it cleared the way for a revenue-generating residential community (Desfor 1993).

After the plan was released, however, the proposed site for the relocated airport, south of the existing airport, was found to have flight paths that interfered with those of the Toronto International Airport (Hodge 1972, 212). The solution was to move the airport to a location off the Eastern Beaches. The proposal became an immediate flashpoint with residents of the Beaches neighbourhood, which was undergoing accelerated gentrification at the time. The large-scale residential community envisioned to replace the airport was itself the source of considerable disagreement due to its cost and its linkage with the larger question of the future of the island airport. The Harbour Commission's original proposal for the site included massive residential development to generate funds for waterfront conversion (Desfor, Goldrick, and Merrens 1989, 491). When the provincial government championed plans for a scaled-down version of Harbour City, the financial implications of this new plan were left unresolved (Province of Ontario, Department of Trade & Development 1970). With a change in provincial leadership as Premier Bill Davis succeeded John Robarts, the plan for a residential community at the airport site was discarded in favour of a proposed Short Take Off and Landing (STOL) service at the existing island airport. Senior government interference effectively ended Metro Toronto's attempts at producing a comprehensive waterfront plan.

Most ambitious and modernist of all were plans for the northern portion of the waterfront site proposed by Metro Centre Ltd, a consortium set up by the Canadian National and Canadian Pacific railway companies to promote the development of their land holdings located between Union Station and the Gardiner Expressway. The Metro Centre concept was formulated in 1968 and submitted to the City of Toronto in 1970. It envisioned office and residential towers set on podiums, diagonal street patterns, the erection of the world's highest tower, and the demolition of Union Station, to be replaced by office towers (Community Development Consultants Ltd 1968; Greenberg 1996; Metropolitan Toronto Planning Board 1970). After intense lobbying from the Metro Centre development team, the city approved the plan without giving much attention to how it fit within the overall waterfront planning effort (Desfor, Goldrick, and Merrens 1989, 492). Central features of the plan, such as the demolition of Union Station, raised massive opposition and the cost of rail relocation proved to be prohibitive (Greenberg 1996). Ultimately, the entire project, with the exception of its centerpiece, the CN Tower, was abandoned.

A new crop of proposals for the rail lands appeared in the 1980s, though this time the rail companies focused on their own respective properties. CN Realty, then the property development division of CN Rail, focused on a district to the west of the CN Tower, now known as CityPlace. Like the Metro Centre proposal, secondary planning revolved around a centrepiece, which helped solidify political support. The SkyDome, a large stadium with a retractable roof (since renamed the Rogers Centre), was a provincial initiative. The entire Rail Lands Secondary Plans received council approval in 1986. Only the stadium was completed immediately, as the remaining area was subject to a holding designation, which required further planning review. The delay allowed the council's left-wing members, who saw a resurgence in their fortunes in the 1988 municipal election, to mount a campaign against the proposal. As much of the area was slated for high-rise commercial buildings, detractors saw this as a collapse of the Central Area Plan, one of the key legacies of the earlier 1970s reform movement. Likewise, council's left-wing members demanded that more provisions be made for affordable housing. Protracted negotiations and review at the Ontario Municipal Board ultimately resulted in added amenities. However, the actual development of the rail lands was once again stalled with the onset of the early-1990s recession.

Harbourfront: The Planning and the Reality

The original redevelopment concept for Harbourfront, the portion of the waterfront to the west of Harbour Square, involved the creation of a park. But the concept gradually evolved into a mixture of park space and cultural activities, as well as commercial and residential developments intended to provide financial support for the cultural activities. The presence of affordable housing was given prominence as Toronto was confronted with a worsening housing crisis in the 1980s. Harbourfront received the most attention on the Toronto waterfront because of its size, its strategic location along the lake and close to downtown, the extent of its redevelopment, its numerous cultural activities, and perhaps above all, the intensity of the opposition its development triggered.

The Ministry of State for Urban Affairs had the initial mandate for Harbourfront's development. However, it had limited success in coordinating Harbourfront's planning and development processes. After several years of negotiations and unsuccessful attempts at launching development, including the formation of a local development council, a new development corporation was set up. Created in 1976, the Harbourfront Corporation was a nine-member federal Crown corporation given responsibility for the development of the entire project and its programming, and allowed to hire and fire the management team (Fraser 1976). While formally Ottawa appointed the board, control of the corporation rested in the hands of local appointees and planners. Two appointees came from the city, two from Metro, and the remaining five through agreement between these two agencies and Ottawa.

Incremental steps had been previously taken to physically open the site to the public and begin cultural programming. However, despite years of negotiation and extensive public consultation, there was a lack of consensus amongst decision-makers over the larger objectives (Gordon 1994, 6–8). Harbourfront became a favoured destination for former city planning staff and influential planners. The agency changed the direction of the project from a recreational area that integrated existing buildings to a commercial-residential district capable of generating sufficient revenue to financially support a wide range of cultural activities. In effect, the earlier vision of a park within Harbourfront had been replaced by plans for an animated and diverse cultural centre, dependent for its financing on profitable on-site private development (Miller 1979). A development framework was produced, with the stated goal being to "preserve and develop Harbourfront as a public place" as well as to "account for its special location, conditions and history," all while achieving financial self-sufficiency (Harbourfront Corporation 1978, 7). Central to all this was the presence of affordable residential and commercial districts to "generate an all day, year-round population" (Harbourfront Corporation 1978, 8). As was to be expected, the linkage between development and cultural funding at the heart of the Harbourfront concept caused tensions between development and the public's desire for open space.

Conceptual renderings depicted several buildings. They appeared to be fewer than eight stories and were interwoven with parks and other recreational areas. The presence of a residential building on the waterfront guaranteed a year-round population as well as a revenue stream required to support cultural activities. Planners styled the project as an extension of the urban fabric, but with much more open space than in the central parts of the city (Best 1977).

History repeated itself in 1979 when the federal Liberals again attempted to use Harbourfront as a gift to Toronto in the context of an electoral campaign. They pledged full funding for the project based on the prevailing conceptual framework (*Globe and Mail* 1979). Once more, the promise failed to deliver electoral support. The Progressive Conservatives took twelve of Metro's twenty-three seats, up from five, and became a minority government (Palango 1979).

Like the Liberals before them, the Progressive Conservatives lauded the project, but they also expressed concern about its cost (Dineen 1979). Meanwhile the concept received approval from the new chief planning commissioner as well as from city council, on the grounds that not only was much of its housing going to be affordable but that thirty percent of the housing stock was to be subsidized as non-profit co-op rent-supplement and rent-geared-to-income units. In an ironic reversal of roles, typically anti-development councillors such as John Sewell (by then the mayor) and Alan Sparrow defended the concept, while the Board of Trade, the Redevelopment Advisory Council, and the railway companies objected, ostensibly because the project would ruin the idea of a park, but perhaps more fundamentally because the publicly funded project was a possible source of competition as well as a potential obstruction to valuable views of the lake (Stein 1979).

During their brief stint in power, the Progressive Conservatives worked behind the scenes to develop a master plan for the area. Upon the Liberals' return to power, the new Public Works minister, Paul Cosgrove, became a strong supporter of the plan, and worked to win over dissenters within the cabinet and to secure Treasury Board approval (Dalby 1980). His work paid off, as on 13 June 1980 the federal government approved a $25 million contribution to the project. The remaining $200 million required for the development was to be provided by private investments (Rickwood and Mietkiewicz 1980). Significantly, the federal government affirmed that it would not make any further contribution. After seven years, development revenues were to be sufficient to fully sustain Harbourfront's cultural activities (*Globe and Mail* 1980a; Gordon 1994, 6–16). The project would then be on its own. With the start-up money in place, the city quickly ratified a secondary plan and approved the required zoning by-laws (*Globe and Mail* 1980b).

After its allocation of seed money, the federal government's direct involvement in Harbourfront diminished. Planning was carried out by former city planners, and effective control of the project was now in the hands of City of Toronto and Metro appointees, with development guidelines to be negotiated between Harbourfront and the City of Toronto. While the overall Harbourfront concept was well received, things turned out differently for individual projects and for the form taken by Harbourfront's actual development.

The most notable example of this departure was a low-cost housing development called Harbour Point. A call for proposals went out in the midst of the early-1980s recession. Having lost much of its developable land to requirements for view corridors, roadways, transitways, open space, and policing, the Harbourfront Corporation loaded the density allowed onto the northernmost portion of the site, between the Gardiner Expressway and Queen's Quay West (Gordon 1994, 6–25). The city, in the midst of a housing shortage and administered by a pro-development council, approved the site plan over its planners' objections. Though the project did not breach planning guidelines, critics soon lamented its height and unadorned appearance. It was widely deemed to be undeserving of so prestigious a site as Harbourfront.

Assisted housing became a contentious issue as the federal Conservative government ceased funding new subsidized housing. Thenceforth, it became difficult for Harbourfront to meet its assisted housing targets. To satisfy the requirement for assisted housing, Harbourfront proposed a private project with rents comparable to the city's affordable housing (Kashmeri 1986). Both city planners and the left-wing councillors opposed the stratagem. For them the attempt to designate a private project as "assisted housing" was anathema to the plan's original intent. Chief Planning Commissioner Stephen McLaughlin resisted the move to waive the initial requirement for assisted housing and was especially opposed to the high density proposed for the project (Gooderman 1986). The pro-development city council, led by Mayor Art Eggleton, again ruled against its planners and gave the go-ahead. McLaughlin resigned by year's end to take on a review of federal properties on the Toronto waterfront (Radkewycz 1986).

Overall, in its rush for financial self-sufficiency, the Harbourfront Corporation promoted a rapid development of its land, favouring in the process financial gain over design principles and its affordable housing obligations. It seemed that financial imperatives were far more important to the Harbourfront Corporation than the presence of affordable housing or adherence to planning principles.

Harbourfront came under attack from different fronts. First, affluent and politically connected residents moving into the new Harbourfront luxury condominiums were overwhelmed with a pace and scale of development that exceeded what they had been led to anticipate, and lamented a lack of amenities (Taylor 1987). Second, because Harbourfront was not producing parks and open spaces at an acceptable rate, the city's parks commissioner called for a development freeze (Stein 1987). There was disagreement over the definition of "open space." Original plans had called for twenty acres of park space and twenty acres of other open space. At issue was the categorization by Harbourfront of small residual spaces surrounding buildings as open space (Gordon 1994, 6–33). Momentum built for a transformation of all remaining space into parks. Third, the political leadership had changed at the local, regional, and provincial levels. Social democrats became a much stronger force on city council in 1988. A Liberal, Alan Tonks, took over the chair of Metro Toronto, a position typically held by a Conservative, and the provincial Progressive Conservatives were defeated in 1985 and replaced by the Liberals. What is more, Harbourfront's direct lobbying of City of Toronto politicians strained its relationship with the city planning department.

City council, followed by the federal government, imposed development freezes in order to perform reviews. When severe crises would flare, the federal government would abandon its arm's-length approach and intervene directly. The city worked on a compromise, and city councillors ratified a new plan believing they had struck a balance between the need for additional open space and the revenue requirements of the Harbourfront Corporation. But the province stepped into the debate in 1990 by imposing its own development freeze, which, given the need for the Harbourfront Corporation to rely on further development for its financial survival, sounded its death knell.

Over these years, the THC, facing a financial crisis due to declining port activity, was also trying to generate revenues by selling land to non-industrial activities (Royal Commission on the Future of the Toronto Waterfront 1989b, 47). An aggressive land-development program by the THC was endorsed by pro-development councillors over the objections of their left-leaning counterparts and of planners (Laver 1981). Several deals were made, the largest being the World Trade Centre development. By the mid-1980s, exemptions from the stipulations of Toronto's Central Area Plan had become commonplace for large developments, and the World Trade Centre was allowed a density that exceeded secondary plan prescriptions by twenty-one percent. Also the city accepted $2 million in lieu of an affordable housing requirement (Taylor 1986). The project was easily approved by council (17–4), despite the opposition of leftist councillors.

The second phase was marked by a simultaneous decline in the industrial vocation of the waterfront and rising interest on the part of the public, politicians, and developers in a transformation of the sector. There was, however, an absence of consensus among these constituencies, as well as between levels of governments, around the form waterfront redevelopment should take. The federal government, which owned most of the land, had a determining influence on waterfront redevelopment over this period. Mostly without heeding City of Toronto and Metro Toronto planning processes, the federal government itself and the agency it set up made decisions that resulted in what was widely perceived as over-development. As it turned out, waterfront redevelopment reflected the federal government's financial priorities and the coincidence between these objectives and those of developers intent on maximizing the scale of development.

IMPLEMENTATION IN THE FACE OF CRITICISM
(FROM THE 1980S ONWARDS)

This last phase is characterized by attempts to revise the approach to waterfront redevelopment in the face of widespread protest against high density, insufficient public open space, and the poor architectural quality of many projects. The third phase illustrates the limited impact public opinion had on the trajectory of waterfront development. It is through the course of the third phase, while strong reactions against the over-development of the waterfront were voiced, that the bulk of the redevelopment has taken place, much of it in the form of high-rise condominium buildings. While the beginning of this phase can be set in the 1980s, it represents the culmination of movements originating in the early 1970s.

Uncoordinated Development

Rapidly, Harbour Square and especially Metro Centre came to represent the epitome of modernist architecture and planning, which were quickly falling out of favour. These developments flew in the face of the urban vision – and its waterfront variant – which was promoted by a rising coalition of urban reformers, mostly middle-class residents and some more radical elements. In Toronto, the expression "reformer" was generally associated with a group of councillors who first took office in the early 1970s and who were opposed to a pro-development old-guard (Caulfield 1974; Sewell 1972). In reality, these reformers were reflecting changing values among inner-city residents, associated with an increasing presence of well-educated citizens. The perspective to which reformers adhered involved the protection of traditional inner-city neighbourhoods and the creation of new small-scale neighbourhoods with a mixed-use, walking orientation. The St Lawrence neighbourhood, whose development had begun in the early 1970s, perhaps best conformed to this vision. It consisted of mid-rise apartment structures with retail at ground level to assure street activity. And just as important, the neighbourhood included a high proportion of subsidized housing to foster a socially mixed environment. City of Toronto planners had consulted extensively with the noted urbanist Jane Jacobs throughout the planning of the St Lawrence neighbourhood, hence its reflection of the urban principles found in her writing.

Members of the urban reformers coalition favoured the creation of plentiful park space along the waterfront. Emboldened by their success in stopping the Spadina Expressway, a majority slate of reform candidates was elected in 1972, and thus assumed control over municipal policy-making (Donald 2002, 2139). There was also concern about undue developer influence on the different agencies responsible for the waterfront. Developers indeed appeared to have their way, with adverse consequences for the planning of the waterfront and the availability of public space. A more current source of contention is the evolution of the waterfront into a residential ghetto for small and high-income households, a consequence of the proliferation of high-rise condominium buildings. It is important to note that the views expressed by urban reformers were widely shared by the population as a whole, which too was of the opinion that densities were too high and that not enough of the waterfront was given to public space.

The exceptional appeal of certain waterfront sites for residential, hotel, and recreational uses was a source of considerable pressure for piecemeal redevelopment. City planners, who had relaunched central waterfront comprehensive planning following the political failure of the ambitious THC/Metro plan, had difficulty meeting their objectives. An extensive process was begun in 1972, the goal of which was to plan for an integrated vision for the city's waterfront while coordinating the actions of the many governing agencies involved (City of Toronto 1974). According to former planners, this process provided an opportunity for a sustained effort to overcome the institutional resistance that had undermined previous initiatives (Interview 2). However, the process was cumbersome, involving dozens of public agencies and stakeholders in planning and technical committees working on long-term (up to thirty-year) development planning, while also accounting for current demands (Desfor, Goldrick, and Merrens 1989, 492). Like the previous Metro Toronto effort, the city-led comprehensive planning process had difficulty delivering desired outcomes within such an institutionally complex environment. More insidiously, the financial opportunities and demands arising from development industry interest in the waterfront increased exponentially, leaving the more abstract and long-term planning effort at the mercy of immediate concerns and the ambitions of city councillors and private developers.

While generally committed to growth control in downtown Toronto and the preservation of established neighbourhoods, reformers acknowledged the strong development potential of the waterfront (Toronto Planning Board 1977a). The reformist council extensively modified the official plan but maintained the potential for development in the central harbour and allowed for the creation of the St Lawrence neighbourhood on former industrial lands just north of the waterfront (Toronto Planning Board 1977b). Likewise, with a development framework and start-up money from the federal government, the city quickly ratified a secondary plan and approved zoning by-laws for Harbourfront, thus short-circuiting its own comprehensive waterfront planning process launched in 1972 (Toronto Planning Department 1980).

Given the protracted nature of this process, it was inevitable that individual projects would be approved before the release of the final recommendations, which took place in 1984. It had proven impossible to formulate a consistent policy for the entire waterfront, as the most significant projects were negotiated and approved separately. The resulting impression that waterfront redevelopment was unfolding in an uncoordinated fashion was a major factor in the involvement of both the federal and provincial governments in a review process. City council approval of the recommendations emanating from the 1972–84 planning process was not granted until 1988, at which time the entire waterfront redevelopment process had become the object of the federal-provincial Royal Commission on the Future of the Toronto Waterfront – the Crombie Commission (City of Toronto Planning & Development Department 1991).

The Toronto Harbour Commission, previously responsible for the Metropolitan Plan, was especially recalcitrant to adopt broader objectives that did not fit its own ambitions (Interview 1). It perceived its role as the encouragement of the development of its land, much of the waterfront, so as to stem the city's loss of industry as well as to generate new areas of mixed use. However, the THC's institutional style made it difficult for it to deal with other agencies, contributing to failed negotiations for an industrial park on the port lands (Desfor 1993, 174).

The development approach of the THC and the resulting land uses were contested by an eclectic mix of environmentalists, housing advocates, boaters, waterfront residents, and heritage associations (Hartmann 1999; Royal Commission on the Future of the Toronto Waterfront 1990, 202–3). But above all, the THC was targeted by pro- and anti-development councillors alike for alleged improprieties in the 1986 sale of Marine Terminal 27 at the foot of Yonge Street (Interview 2). City council demanded that the THC restart the bidding process (Fine 1986; Kerr 1986a, 1986b). Refusal to renegotiate the deal brought the Commission under sustained criticism in the media. Although council resisted calls to impeach the sitting directors, their terms in office were not renewed, and they were replaced by city councillors (Monsebraaten 1987).

Attempts at a New Approach

Overall, there is no doubt that the trajectory taken by the development of Harbourfront was the major source of controversy and played the primary role in a revision of the approach to waterfront redevelopment.

In 1986, the federal Conservative government launched a Task Force on Program Review. In its report on federal real property, the Nielsen Task Force recommended the classification of federal lands into two categories – required and surplus – and also recommended that the federal government divest itself of surplus lands (Government of Canada and Nielsen Task Force on Program Review 1985). Under the impetus of the City of Toronto and in response to widespread criticism about the nature of waterfront development, in 1987 the city's former planning commissioner, Stephen McLaughlin, performed an evaluation of federal property on the Toronto waterfront. The McLaughlin report concurred with the Nielsen report's proposed overhaul of the federal government's land management process, and recommended a review of the Harbourfront Corporation and the Toronto Harbour Commission (McLaughlin 1987). A major problem highlighted by the McLaughlin report concerned the fragmentation of waterfront properties among several agencies and the absence of coordination among these agencies. It recommended that the federal and provincial governments form a special committee on the Toronto waterfront, and the following year, just such a committee was established. This committee quickly became a full federal Royal Commission, which was accompanied a year later by a concurrent provincial Royal Commission. The two commissions operated jointly.

The Royal Commission on the Future of the Toronto Waterfront attempted to unravel the complicated web of conflicts between the various agencies and actors. Among its many recommendations, the Commission advocated separating the cultural and transportation functions of Harbourfront and the Toronto Harbour Commission, respectively, from their land-development activities (Royal Commission on the Future of the Toronto Waterfront 1989a). It also proposed a new land-management regime to help bring in new industries, while also opening several areas for mixed use (Royal Commission on the Future of the Toronto Waterfront 1991). On advice from the head of the Royal Commission and former mayor, David Crombie (see Desfor 1993), three city councillors used their majority on the THC to transfer land to the City of Toronto Economic Development Corporation (TEDCO) (Tassé 2006, 15). After several years of internal division on city council, another land transfer was completed, with all the lands transferred totalling approximately 250 hectares.

The federal Liberals continued the land divestiture process and privatized the national railway, Canadian National. A non-agent (that is, independent from the federal government from a decision-making and liability perspective) Crown corporation, the Canada Lands Company, was given responsibility for divesting CN railway lands to developers. On the Toronto waterfront, the railway lands were sold to a private developer in the mid-1990s and the CN Tower was leased (Wong 1997). The Canada Lands Company later reassumed operational responsibility for the CN Tower (Wong 2003).

Reduced Federal Land Ownership and the Creation of the Toronto Port Authority

By the mid-1990s, much of the federal government's waterfront lands had been sold or ceded to other levels of government. As part of an ongoing refocusing of its activities, the federal government introduced a process for divesting itself of its responsibility for ports. A new act was proposed which applied to eight of Canada's trade significant ports (Government of Canada 1996). The proposed Canada Marine Act had been intended to create port authorities for large financially self-sustainable ports, not regional ports such as Toronto (Moloney 1996). Consultants investigated the viability of the Toronto port along with other candidate ports. Like earlier research on the matter, the study found that the Port of Toronto was not self-sustainable, and would thus require an ongoing operational subsidy (Booz, Allen, and Hamilton 1992; Mariport Group Ltd 1999; Royal Commission on the Future of the Toronto Waterfront 1989a).

The inclusion of the Toronto port among those ports that were worthy of federal attention and the 1999 creation of the Toronto Port Authority (TPA) reflected a sentiment among senior Liberal MPs that the federal government should retain a presence on the Toronto waterfront. The Toronto MPs of the time were particularly concerned about the scale of waterfront development that had occurred during the 1980s, though the pro-development mayor of the time was now an MP and indeed president of the Treasury Board (Interview 3). A federal official saw the creation of the TPA in terms of a possible economic development role on the part of the federal government in the Toronto region, and a source of patronage appointments (Interview 3). Senior officials asked consultants to be creative in finding ways to include the port of Toronto among federally significant ports. In the words of an interviewee, they told consultants to "have another go of this. See if we get creative; see if when certain things are done, this can make a profit. So they came back with a positive answer" (Interview 3).

Though federally created, the TPA is an arm's-length agency. It does not take direction from Transport Canada, and the Financial Administration Act does not apply to it (Tassé 2006, 30). It holds very little land besides the airport, the port, and the outer marina. It does not have expropriation rights, cannot overrule the city on issues of land use, and is limited in its ability to borrow, though subsequent legislative amendments allowed for more debt carrying capacity (Pooley and Harding 2003). An important difference with the TPA in terms of governance is that the City of Toronto no longer appoints a majority of delegates, and no politician or civil servant can sit on the board. Instead, of the seven board members, one is appointed by the province, one by the city, one by the federal Transport minister, and the remaining four by the federal Transport minister in consultation with stakeholders from the port, airport, and recreational facilities under the TPA's mandate.

The precariousness of its financial base compelled the TPA to make the most of its assets, one of which was the island airport. By 1994, the province had refused to continue paying for the operation of the airport ferry and the federal government planned to phase out funding to the airport altogether (Campion-Smith 1994). Both governments invoked fiscal conservatism, explaining that the airport had to find a way to become solvent.

The Port Authority pursued the creation of a bridge to the airport as a way of increasing traffic and revenues. The bridge project had received repeated initial approvals from city council during the 1990s, though its realization ultimately required the amendment of an agreement between the City of Toronto, the Port Authority, and Transport Canada. Boosters of the bridge, including the Toronto Board of Trade, focused on the advantages of a readily accessible downtown airport for business along with the benefits of speeding up response times for emergency services (Moloney 2002). A further argument in favour of the bridge was its role in carrying air-transported patients to major Toronto hospitals. City council, led by Mayor Mel Lastman, subscribed to these arguments in favour of the bridge.

The airport and the perceived threat of its expansion has been a contested local planning issue going back a generation (Hodge 1972). The bridge to the airport was a mobilizing political issue for urban reformers after the loss of a great deal of their power base on council following the forced 1998 amalgamation of the City of Toronto. As in previous efforts, reformers were successful in building a coalition with an eclectic mix of interest groups, including environmentalists, academics, boaters, and artists. Most importantly, the areas adjacent to the airport were now thriving residential and commercial districts, and the prospect of greater airport traffic brought focused criticism from local residents.

Among the reformers who opposed the airport were two former mayors, John Sewell and David Crombie, as well as Jane Jacobs. Residents of the Toronto Islands and waterfront conservationists were especially adamant in their objection to the airport plans, and artists using facilities for open-air concerts and the cinema industry, which frequently filmed on the waterfront, were equally concerned about the noise and pollution effects of an expanded airport (Rusk 2002). The strongest voice of dissent came from an organization called Community Airport Impact Review (Community AIR). Adhering to the view of city planning documents that promised a "clean, green, waterfront," it depicted the city's options in stark terms: "As Toronto becomes known for its bad air and increasingly frequent smog days, it is self-evident that the city can have a clean, green waterfront or it can have a busy waterfront airport. It cannot have both" (Community AIR 2007). Some also saw the airport as an impediment to the future development of the waterfront (Wanagas 2002). A Toronto former planner described the conflict at a meeting:

> [U]nder the Lastman regime [the TPA] knew they had the support of the Council on the airport issue and on other issues. I

remember that awful, awful meeting. It went on all day. Seventy-five deputations including Jane Jacobs and Crombie – a joint economic development committee about the island airport and all the rest of it. Oh my god. Bitter. And the vast majority of everybody saying, don't do this for all these reasons … The result was so predictable. They overwhelmingly approved the bridge. And when it went to council, same thing all over again. They knew it was going to pass. So the port authority had the amalgamated council by the short hairs. (Interview 4)

The federal government abided by the decision of city council and signed off on an amendment permitting the construction of a bridge. In the interim, however, the controversy surrounding the bridge and airport had become an issue in the 2003 municipal election. Toronto councillor David Miller differentiated himself from other mayoral candidates by coming out against the bridge and pledging to stop the construction at no cost to the city, and the bridge became the foremost issue of the campaign (Walkom 2003). Miller won the election, and used local endorsement to pressure the federal government to reintroduce a ban on a bridge to the airport, ostensibly to avoid having the city assume liability towards the TPA and airline operators by withdrawing its approvals (Harding 2004). After negotiations, the federal government acquiesced and paid the Port Authority and others affected by the cancellation $35 million (Lewington 2005a; Safieddine and James 2005). A review of the Port Authority's operations under the federal Conservatives was conducted in October 2006. It found no fault with the way the TPA was created and it endorsed its continued operations, though it did suggest that the TPA should take a more open and conciliatory approach (Tassé 2006). Despite the loss of the bridge, the airport operator and the Port Authority persisted with their plans for upgraded service. A new airline based its operation at the airport, though it became involved in a legal dispute with Air Canada, which it dislodged from the airport by taking over the management of the terminal (Gonda 2006).

Recent Institutional Structures and Waterfront Development

As the 1990s progressed and Harbourfront development proceeded apace, there were two development frontiers left on the waterfront. One was the eastern portion of Toronto's central waterfront (including East Bayfront, West Don Lands, and the Port Lands). The area, upheld for several decades for industrial use, was by then considered to be well-suited to post-industrial redevelopment subsequent to the report of the Royal Commission on the Future of the Toronto Waterfront. A Waterfront Trust was assembled to pursue redevelopment, and the City of Toronto recommended the redevelopment of the East Bayfront in its official plan (City of Toronto Planning and Development Department 1993).

Interest in the redevelopment of the eastern section of the waterfront peaked in 1999 during the Toronto bid for the 2008 Olympic Games. David Crombie, former head of the Royal Commission and chair of the Waterfront Trust, helped lead a grassroots campaign, meeting in small groups with a range of stakeholders in an effort to build support and address the community concerns that had undermined a previous Olympic bid (Laidley 2007, 267). An Olympic bid committee was created, representing a large and powerful coalition of financial deal-makers, developers, and bureaucrats, and enjoying overwhelming support from the post-amalgamation city hall (Kipfer and Keil 2002). The Olympic Bid Committee focused its attention on the eastern waterfront. When it was determined that the installations, including the Olympic Village, were to be concentrated on the Port Lands, the committee deemed it essential to have a plan and a strategy for both this area and the entire forty-six-kilometer-long post-amalgamation City of Toronto Waterfront. Mayor Lastman promoted this vision, with the premier and the prime minister both making commitments to the revitalization of the waterfront at a public meeting on November 1999 (Rusk 1999). This expression of support was followed by the report of the Toronto Waterfront Revitalization Task Force (2000) chaired by Robert Fung, a financier with an impressive political network, including direct access to the prime minister. The report called for a development agency dedicated to the redevelopment of the entire waterfront. It would involve the three levels of government. The vision for the waterfront was ambitious: based on \$5 billion in public sector investment originating in equal shares from all three levels of government and \$7 billion from the private sector, it would materialize over a twenty- to twenty-five-year period. Proposals voiced in the report included a decontamination of former industrial land, housing development, improved transit access, and a network of canals.

However, no sooner was the report released than the Toronto Economic Development Corporation (TEDCO) announced it was signing a twenty-year lease with a retailer for a three-hectare property. The anticipated big box store was clearly out of character with the vision of the Task Force for the site. TEDCO went ahead with the deal despite warnings from the chair of the Task Force to avoid long-term commitments for the 170 hectares of waterfront land it owned (James 2000a, 2000b; Lakey 2000; Lakey and Spremo 2000).

In March 2001, the three levels of government announced the creation of an agency, the Toronto Waterfront Revitalization Corporation (TWRC), responsible for redevelopment along the entire City of Toronto Waterfront. The TWRC (now called Waterfront Toronto) was allocated $300 million to launch key projects (Lakey 2001; Welsh and Lakey 2001). The Corporation was headed by Robert Fung and the board was to be constituted of people nominated by the city, province, and federal government, most of whom were not elected representatives or employees of these levels of government (Government of Ontario 2002; Rusk 2001). One of the major purposes of the new agency was to show that Toronto had the organizational capacity to create the Olympic site.

On 13 July 2001, the International Olympic Committee selected Beijing over Toronto for the 2008 games. Despite strong statements to the contrary on the part of politicians, the enduring commitment of the three levels of government to a large-scale revitalization of the waterfront was now in doubt. Another ambitious report was tabled, this time prepared in 2001 by the City of Toronto. The report was organized around twenty-three major interventions, including constructing 40,000 housing units, burying the Gardiner Expressway, creating a continuous green band along the water as well as numerous parks, and building a pier and a plaza at the foot of Yonge Street. However, there was uncertainty about the capacity of the TWRC to achieve these objectives (James 2001). The promised money was slow in coming, as was the transfer of control over lands to the TWRC (Gillespie 2004b; Hume 2002b). By 2004, of the $1.5 billion that had been committed by the three governments, only $35 million had been transferred to the TWRC (Gillespie 2004a; Lewington 2004). And to make matters worse, developments that were inconsistent with the planning vision of the two reports were going ahead on the eastern part of the waterfront: film studios, big box stores, and a power generation plant (Hume 2002a, 2004). Again, TEDCO was defiant of long-term planning objectives.

The fortunes of the TWRC took a turn for the better in the summer of 2004, as the federal and provincial governments allocated $334 million for a number of projects such as the extension of Front Street, improvements to Union Station, an environmental assessment of naturalizing the mouth of the Don River, the remediation of industrial properties in the Port Lands so they could accommodate housing and parks, and a boardwalk along Harbourfront Centre. And with most significance for the eastern part of the waterfront, the province committed to a 6,500-unit residential development, with a large proportion of affordable housing, on the West Don Lands (Gillespie 2006; Lewington 2005b). Under the organizational umbrella of the TWRC, the different levels of government have focused on their own projects. As the province concentrates on the West Don Lands, the City of Toronto is pursuing a mixed-use project on East Bayfront (expected to accommodate 10,000 residents and 8,000 employees) and the federal government is carrying out the development of parks (Interview 5; Toronto Waterfront Revitalization Corporation 2005).

The second development frontier is the railway lands. In an attempt to maximize revenue from their land, railway companies long envisioned devoting most of it to high-rise office development, until recently the most lucrative use by far of land close to downtown. But the height of the proposed buildings and the lack of provision for affordable housing were a constant source of wrangling with the City of Toronto. The railway companies continued to be particularly incompetent in putting their case forward, as when proposing to replace Union Station with high-rise office structures. There was also the matter of the size of the downtown office market. If permitted to fully develop their land, the railway companies could have reproduced several times the amount of office space found in downtown Toronto. Obviously, there was no market to absorb anything close to this amount of office space. This was especially the case since downtown office development had stalled in the early 1990s. In 1996 the Canada Lands Company sought proposals to redevelop the twenty-hectare site (Zehr 1996). Grand Adex Properties (later renamed Concord Adex), which proposed a massive residential project, was the firm selected by the Company (Gibbon 1997; Zehr 1997). Grand Adex, owned by Hong Kong interests, was carrying out at the time a major condominium development on Vancouver's Expo 86 site, which was to serve as a model for the railway lands development. The Vancouver project, consisting of multiple condominium towers, won praise for its street orientation. Once built, CityPlace (the name given to the railway lands project) will consist of seventeen residential towers as well as a number of lower structures. CityPlace will complete the redevelopment of the railway lands, already host to the SkyDome (now Rogers Centre), CN Tower, Toronto Convention Centre, and Air Canada Centre.

If the previous phase was driven by changing expectations about the role of the waterfront, the present phase has been largely shaped by responses to critiques of the first wave of waterfront transformations. A predominant event in this latest historical phase was the retreat of the federal government as a major landholder. As prior conflicts stemmed largely from diverging perspectives between the federal government and Metro Toronto and City of Toronto planning agencies, one could have reasonably expected a more harmonious and better coordinated redevelopment process. Such a situation did not materialize, however. Discord persisted among the different agencies responsible for the waterfront, between levels of government as well as between agencies and governments. While no longer a major landowner, the federal government remained an influential player thanks to its financial resources and its enduring control over the port and the airport.

OUTCOMES

The most striking aspect of the Toronto waterfront redevelopment process is the extremely long time it took. Serious consideration was given to waterfront redevelopment nearly five decades ago, and while sectors closest to downtown are fully redeveloped, eastern portions are still far from this stage.

Another feature of waterfront redevelopment is its fragmentation. Each district within the waterfront is distinguished by its level of redevelopment, functional specialization, and layout. Harbourfront features a mixture of high-density residential land uses, cultural and recreational activities, and some open space, within a built environment that reflects architectural and planning trends that dominated the 1980s and 1990s. Meanwhile, Harbour Square is composed of a mixture of residential towers and a large hotel, whose architecture and layout are consistent with its 1970s planning and development. The railway lands are mostly devoted to housing and with their glass-clad condominium towers celebrate 1990s–2000s architectural styles. Finally, the eastern portion of the waterfront is itself at different stages of development and will present a mixture of uses, including high-rise and medium density residential development, retail and big box stores, and residual industrial and port uses. There is still an absence of pedestrian connectivity between the different parts of the waterfront, and most of the waterfront is separated from the remainder of the city by a ground-level boulevard (Lake Shore Boulevard), an expressway (the Gardiner Expressway), and a railway corridor. As of yet, there is no clear indication of how these obstacles can be overcome (Brook 2007). Perhaps even more serious is a lack of compatibility between land uses. If the mixture of residential, commercial, and recreational uses (as observed in the Harbourfront portion of the waterfront) is currently proclaimed as a sound approach to planning, the juxtaposition of other activities can be more problematic (Cervero and Duncan 2006; Frank, Kavage, and Appleyard 2007; Jabereen 2006; Kenworthy 2006). This is notable in the case of the island airport (renamed Toronto City Centre Airport in 1994 and Billy Bishop Airport in 2009) in close proximity to high-density housing developments, and the adverse attitude towards the airport on the part of area residents. Nearby big box stores, industrial facilities, and residential areas may give rise to similar problems when the eastern portion of the waterfront is fully developed. In particular, the proximity of car-oriented forms of retailing to new medium-density neighbourhoods may spark conflicts in the future.

The desires of the public regarding open space on the waterfront have not been met (e.g. DeMara 1999). Such aspirations are understandable given the absence of an important park within walking distance of the downtown. A large waterfront park would have filled this need. A comparison is often made between the Chicago waterfront, which is largely devoted to parks and other public spaces, and that of Toronto, which is mostly taken by private development. Some parks are planned for the East Bayfront sector of the waterfront, but these will be neither easy to access from downtown, nor of a scale comparable to the Chicago lakefront parks.

A final critique concerns the lack of architectural distinction of many buildings. This concern, which is directed at private developments, is a reflection of the high expectations placed in the redevelopment of this site. Apart from a few especially undistinguished structures, most buildings are representative of the architectural styles marking their period of development. The problem is that this absence of architectural distinction is not seen as satisfactory for such a prestigious site. Still, some waterfront public-sector projects have been acclaimed in architectural circles. This is notably the case of the widely praised transformation of the Queens Quay Terminal building on Harbourfront. The art deco storage shed erected in the late 1920s was converted in 1983 into a multi-use centre comprising retailing (largely oriented to the tourism market), a dance theatre, and office and residential space.

On the positive side, much of the waterfront has been redeveloped and one could argue that the sequential nature of its growth has prevented a homogeneous and likely monotonous development pattern. Moreover, attempts to create a street-focused urban environment have been largely successful in the Harbourfront portion of the waterfront. The street is also served by a light-rail transit line connecting Harbourfront to downtown and the subway system. By virtue of its proximity to the lake and of its cultural activities, Harbourfront has become an attraction for Toronto residents and tourists alike. And high-density housing has fostered street-level stores and services aimed at residents.

FACTORS OF INFLUENCE

We now turn to factors responsible for the direction taken by the Toronto waterfront redevelopment and for its outcomes. The main focus is on the role played by the federal government. But we first examine other factors in order to set the context in which federal interventions took place, and demonstrate that federal involvement was only one among many diverse influences on waterfront redevelopment.

At a broad scale, Toronto waterfront redevelopment is associated with a society-wide transition from industrialism to post-industrialism (Bell 1999; Kumar 1995; Perloff 1980; Savitch 1988). The post-industrial transition reverberated on the Toronto waterfront in different fashions, all of which proved favourable to its redevelopment. The advent of post-industrialism reduced the potential for industrial development while enhancing consumption-oriented activities, including retailing, the hospitality sector, cultural and recreational activities, and high-density housing. Much of the industrial land became redundant and therefore available for other uses. But the passage from an industrial to a post-industrial use demanded a profound transformation of the sites, involving, among other things, the replacement or thorough retrofitting of existing structures. For areas to function as consumption spaces, they must attract people and thus appeal to the public, a requirement of little concern for industrial spaces. The effect of post-industrialism on the Toronto waterfront was felt at different levels. Not only was the societal transition to post-industrialism responsible for the availability of former industrial land for other uses, but it was also instrumental in the widespread adoption of consumerist lifestyles. Travel, culture, and recreation, towards which many of the new waterfront activities are oriented, figure prominently among features of spreading post-industrial lifestyles.

The post-industrial transition was felt most acutely in inner-city areas, such as the Toronto waterfront. With its proximity to the lake and to downtown Toronto, the waterfront provided amenity and accessibility attributes favourable to post-industrial activities. Toronto waterfront redevelopment must be seen in the context of the gentrification of the old City of Toronto over the last four decades. This area has been and is still being redeveloped to accommodate small and relatively wealthy households with a taste for urban lifestyles. The nature of waterfront redevelopment is largely consistent with this tendency. Yet the presence of an expressway, itself a consequence of attempts to accommodate consumerism in the 1950s, casts a shadow on pedestrian accessibility and the amenity advantages of the waterfront.

The waterfront's evolution was primarily driven by the agencies created to administer different aspects of its development and redevelopment. It reflects a history of organizations following their own mandates and attempting to maximize their respective organizational interests. To be sure, at different times, individual actors did have a determining influence on key decisions and their outcomes – David Crombie's role in the Royal Commission on the waterfront comes immediately to mind, but so does David Miller, along with the planners and developers who have shaped major waterfront developments. However, overall, individuals respected the institutional imperatives of their respective agencies and subscribed to their values. Individuals operating within these organizations harmonized their personal interests with those of their agency, which caused them to attempt to maximize its benefits, possibly at the expense of the objectives of other agencies or political administrations. This is how a former City of Toronto planner (Interview 4) put it in the case of the THC: "I always found it interesting that, when councillors were appointed to the former Harbour Commission, they could have a speech at council, and as soon as they were sitting at the Harbour Commission's table, they were different persons. And they would argue against what they said at council. You know, it was like a private club."

On the other hand, directors have a fiduciary duty to uphold the organization's mandate. The apparent conflict highlighted by Interviewee 4 was addressed in part in the establishment of the Toronto Port Authority under the Canada Marine Act of 1998, where directors cannot be appointed if they are elected representatives or appointed officials from any level of government.

Fundamentally, the history of the development of the Toronto waterfront is largely about the influence on policy-making of institutional architecture – the presence of different levels of government and semi-autonomous agencies, as well as the organizational structures of these agencies (Barley and Tolbert 1997; Clarke 1995; Lecours 2005; March and Olsen 1984). We have seen that the approval of development projects on the waterfront often stemmed from the need on the part of these agencies to balance their budgets, and that financial urgency generally overrode planning objectives. The former Toronto Harbour Commission, for example, sold or rented land for industrial purposes in an attempt to finance its port operation and land reclamation. In the words of a former THC Board member (Interview 1): "So how do you repay your debt? The only way is you look at your properties and you say 'Why do we have them and what use are we going to put them to?' If there is no use foreseen, that's not going to hurt the commission both financially and morally, you sell it! Same as you do if you are a private business." Similarly, the Harbourfront Corporation, showing foremost a commitment to its cultural mandate, pursued an aggressive real estate development strategy to generate the funding required to support its mission.

The central role of agencies in the waterfront redevelopment process was also responsible for its fragmented nature. Each agency pursued its own objectives, often with little regard for those of other agencies. A former City of Toronto planner (Interview 4) described the waterfront administrative fragmentation thusly: "I counted them one time, and there is something like sixteen agencies on the waterfront, and they all have their own agenda. And they all think their ideas are the right way to go. And of course, they have their own rules, own mechanisms and all that."

And in the words of an executive of the TPA: "[The waterfront] is nothing but bumping jurisdictions and difficulties" (Interview 6). The most blatant example of contradictory objectives is the presence of the City Centre (now Billy Bishop) Airport, and the TPA's call for its expansion at the very time that high-density residential development was proceeding apace on nearby portions of the waterfront. In a similar vein, TEDCO gave precedence to its land revenue generation and short-term employment creation objectives over the broad planning vision for the waterfront when it leased strategic land for big box stores.

Also important is the world view of agencies. Each sees the waterfront according to its respective mission and organizational interests. For example, for the TPA it is essential to maintain a port function on the Port Lands for the economic wellbeing of Toronto as well as for environmental reasons. A transshipment of maritime freight from seafaring to Great Lakes vessels, as advocated by the TPA, would reduce dependence on trains and especially environmentally damaging trucking, and give renewed prominence to the Toronto port. Even with its present functions, which are limited to sugar, salt, aggregate, and concrete, the TPA is quick to stress that the harbour diverts 30,000 trucks from Toronto highways (Interview 6). Clearly, these views are in direct contradiction with attempts to replace port functions with housing or commercial or recreational development. TEDCO also illustrates this phenomenon. Its world view, which reflects its mandate, is driven by short-term development and job creation objectives. Little wonder that in its perspective the immediate development of a film studio and of big box stores takes precedence over a planning vision with a twenty-five-year horizon.

FEDERAL PRESENCE

Originally, the federal presence on the waterfront was consistent with the port and railway orientation of the sector, both functions being under federal jurisdiction. Later, as the importance of these uses declined and the focus turned to non-industrial activities, federal government interventions were derived from its ownership of much of the waterfront land. Finally, with the federal government divesting itself of virtually all its land on the waterfront, its involvement in matters related to this sector became justified by its spending capacity, the possible political rewards stemming from a strong presence in Toronto, and its potential economic development role.

If the central role of semi-autonomous agencies stands out in the Toronto waterfront development process, their importance is in large part a function of the involvement of the federal government. Because of a need to assure the participation of other levels of government in decision-making and the lack of land use planning expertise at the federal level, it was difficult for the federal government to intervene directly; hence its reliance on semi-autonomous agencies.

The federal government played an important part in the creation of four agencies that have had major influences on the development of the waterfront: the Toronto Harbour Commission (replaced by the Toronto Port Authority), the Harbourfront Corporation, the Canada Lands Company, and the Toronto Waterfront Revitalization Corporation (later Waterfront Toronto). Each of these agencies was set up as an institutional instrument intended to address specific issues. The goal of the Toronto Harbour Commission was to operate the port while creating and selling industrial land. Its successor, the Toronto Port Authority, was to operate the port and the City Centre Airport, and less specifically, to assure a federal presence on the waterfront. For its part, the Harbourfront Corporation was set up to redevelop the portion of the waterfront under its responsibility in a fashion that would generate funding for cultural activities. The mandate of the Canada Lands Company was the least ambiguous; it was simply to sell railway lands at the highest price. The most ambitious was the objective of the Toronto Waterfront Revitalization Corporation, which was mandated to coordinate the redevelopment of all the City of Toronto waterfront and in the process administer the large sums committed by the three levels of government for this purpose.

In all cases, with the exception of the Canada Lands Company, whose board is nationwide and nominated by the federal government, the federal and municipal (and occasionally regional) levels shared the governance of agencies, as reflected in the composition of their boards of governors. The THC, TPA, and Harbourfront shared a requirement for financial self-reliance. Once more the Canada Lands

Company stands out because its mission was to maximize revenues from the sale of surplus federal land. The TWRC was set up to manage ongoing investments from the federal, provincial, and municipal levels. Also, in all instances except the TWRC, other policy objectives took a distant second place to financial imperatives. Notably, the secondary importance attributed to land use planning in the mandate of agencies can be traced back to the lack of responsibility for such matters at the federal level. This was passed on to the agencies the federal government created. Things were different for the TWRC, whose very purpose was tied to the implementation of a planning vision for the waterfront and whose existence was the outcome of the high-profile involvement of the three levels of government.

Reliance on semi-autonomous agencies prevented the federal government from achieving a fine control of waterfront development. Once set up with their respective mandates and organizational structures, these agencies acquired a momentum of their own. We have seen how, on different occasions, developments yielding financial rewards for the agencies were approved, despite their lack of consistency with planning principles and broader social objectives. What is more, reliance on semi-autonomous agencies made it difficult for the federal government, as well as for other levels of government, to adapt to the changing circumstances on the Toronto waterfront. Agencies tended to maintain their courses of action as dictated by their mandates and organizational structures even in the face of changing circumstances, a behaviour that is understandable since their organizational structures shielded them from the reactions of the public. This is how a former Toronto city councillor (Interview 7) describes the TPA:

> The TPA was designed to remove democratic accountability explicitly. The Liberals, when they set it up, specifically precluded by regulation the participation of any elected official on that body. And the result is that we have a completely unaccountable entity. Unaccountable to the minister – the minister says it is arm's length. Unaccountable to the public, and the result is they have stonewalled any reasonable development of the Waterfront with everything from legal action to irresponsible spending of money on things that clearly the people of Toronto do not want to see such as the expansion of an airport on the Toronto waterfront.

At different times in the history of waterfront development, the federal government felt pressure to modify the trajectory of the agencies it had created. Their behaviours had become inconsistent with a changing economic context, or with mounting public dissatisfaction with the outcomes of waterfront redevelopment, which translated into political pressure for a change of direction. But, because of the varied origins of members on boards of governors and in some cases their requirement to achieve financial autonomy, it was difficult for the federal government to directly influence decisions taken by agencies. A federal official described his relations with the TPA in the following terms: "Even if I did not agree [with a TPA decision] I would not have interfered, because that would not have been appropriate, unless there was a massive public policy issue that had to be resolved … I suppose you could always use the letters patent to do that as an order. But once you do that … you undermine the efficacy of the board, and certainly in the case of airport authorities, the money markets would see this as political influence and therefore would think twice about putting up money." The alternative was then to create new agencies to tackle emerging issues, as in the cases of the Harbourfront Corporation and the TWRC, or to replace an existing agency with a new one, as when the Toronto Port Authority replaced the Toronto Harbour Commission. Thus, over the history of the waterfront, federal influence was felt mostly through the creation of institutional structures, which explains the intermittent presence of the federal government on the Toronto waterfront scene. Most of the time, the federal government was content to let its agencies operate on their own, but when there was a perceived need or crisis, it set up new agencies or replaced existing ones.

Clearly current concerns about the waterfront have resulted, in part, from both federal and municipal institutional structures. Both levels of government created semi-autonomous agencies to address contemporary concerns, only to subsequently find that these agencies' adherence to their founding mandates generated difficulties in the face of changing economic, social, and environmental contexts.

CONCLUSION

The Toronto waterfront provides a clear illustration of the transition from industrial to post-industrial forms of urbanization. It was strategically placed to take advantage of the early phases of industrial development thanks to the presence of port facilities and main railway lines, access to water, and proximity to central parts of the city. But from the 1950s on, the waterfront lost much of its old economic relevance, affected as it was by an overall de-industrialization trend, compounded by the tendency for manufacturing to be lured to suburban sites, and by a marginalization of port operations. Portions of the waterfront enjoyed amenity (presence of the lake) and accessibility (proximity to downtown) advantages that made them highly appealing to growing economic sectors: tourism, cultural and recreational activities, and high-density residential development. These conditions stimulated the transformation of the waterfront from an industrial to a post-industrial environment.

This chapter has documented how this transition from industrial to post-industrial unfolded from the 1950s onwards. It has shown that far from being an automatic response to broad economic trends, the transformation of the waterfront was the outcome of difficult interactions between levels of governments and of a complex dynamic between semi-autonomous agencies that were created to manage different aspects of the waterfront.

Federal dependence on semi-autonomous agencies helped to shape waterfront development dynamics. We have traced the importance of agencies' pursuit of their respective organizational interests. The priorities of agencies have repeatedly clashed with broad, integrated plans advanced by the municipal and regional governments. Self-interested agencies can also be considered responsible for deficient waterfront development coordination.

But it would be wrong to lay the full blame for difficulties in adhering to social objectives and comprehensive planning at the door of the federal government and its agencies. The bypassing of planning processes also happened at the municipal level when pro-development councils approved projects before plans were finalized or despite their lack of conformity with prevailing planning objectives. Moreover, the City of Toronto also made use of semi-autonomous agencies, with consequences similar to those associated with federally mandated agencies. The Toronto Economic Development Corporation (TEDCO), a municipal creation, adopted an approach similar to that of the other agencies by developing lands with a short-term economic development perspective. While consistent with its mandate, this approach often flies in the face of longer-term goals. For example, TEDCO, as a separate entity set up under provincial legislation, resisted a request from the city to transfer lands to the TWRC. In the end, the city had to resort to a shareholder declaration – the city being its only shareholder – to compel TEDCO to transfer lands.

However, the nature of the often tortuous waterfront administrative environment was largely a consequence of the federal government's involvement, given its responsibility for port operations and, for much of the twentieth century, its status as principal landowner. It was because of the federal government's need to ensure the influence of locally based, usually municipal, interests on waterfront-related decisions that it relied on semi-autonomous agencies to manage this district's development. These agencies were initially established to advance federal objectives for the waterfront. But these semi-autonomous agencies came to be driven by their own organizational interests and subsequently proved to be resistant to changes in economic and social circumstances. The central role given to agencies hampered efforts to achieve a coordinated approach to waterfront development and caused clashes with planning objectives throughout the post-industrial redevelopment phase. As a rule, agencies gave priority to their own financial imperatives over longer-term goals, thus becoming land development promoters. In this context, the federal presence was to a large extent confined to the creation or replacement of its agencies. Although this arrangement did not allow the federal government to exercise a direct influence on waterfront development, it nonetheless permitted it to set broad orientations.

Today, the waterfront is largely redeveloped, much of it occupied by high-rise buildings, with a relatively small proportion of its space given to parks and other public areas. The waterfront contains conflicting land uses and as yet there is little interconnection among its different sectors. These present land use patterns on the Toronto waterfront can be traced back to a complex and divisive administrative setup. This is especially the case for the Harbourfront and Harbour Square portions of the waterfront, which many perceive as overbuilt, and for the railway lands, which are currently undergoing intense high-rise condominium development. Also associated with the role of semi-autonomous agencies is the fragmented nature of waterfront development in the absence of an overarching planning concept. The shift to new urbanism, a municipal planning objective, was not adopted by other waterfront agencies. There are instances of incompatible land uses and an absence of pedestrian connectivity across the entire waterfront. Urban planning approaches reflecting a public desire for a comprehensive, accessible, and attractive waterfront were often set aside in the face of financial gain from land development, to the detriment of an overall, comprehensive approach to the planning and redevelopment of this vital piece of Canada's urban waterfront lands.

INTERVIEWS

1 Former THC board member and general manager. Toronto, 19 July 2007.
2 Former planner. Toronto, 26 July 2007.
3 Federal official. 27 July 2007.
4 Former planner. Toronto, 18 July 2007.
5 TWRC board member. Toronto, 25 July 2007.
6 TPA executive. Toronto, 9 July 2007.
7 Former Toronto city councillor. 7 September 2007.
8 Former executive, Toronto Economic Development Corporation. Toronto, 13 July 2007.
9 Executive, Toronto Waterfront Secretariat. Toronto, 17 May 2007.
10 Former researcher, Royal Commission on the Future of the Toronto Waterfront. Toronto, 19 July 2007.
11 Planner, Canada Lands. 19 September 2007
12 Planner, Canada Lands. 19 September 2007.

REFERENCES

Bacher, John C. 1993. *Keeping to the Marketplace: The Evolution of Canadian Housing Policy*. Montreal & Kingston: McGill-Queen's University Press.

Barley, S.R., and Pamela S. Tolbert. 1997. "Institutionalization and Structuration: Structuring the Links between Action and Institution." *Organizational Studies* 18: 93–117.

Bell, Daniel. 1999. *The Coming of Post-Industrial Society: A Venture in Social Forecasting*. New York: Basic Books.

Booz, Allen, and Hamilton. 1992. *Organizational Plan and Budgets for the Toronto Harbour Commission: Final Report*. Toronto: Toronto Harbour Commissioners and Toronto Economic Development Corporation.

Brook, C. 2007. "Elevating the Gardiner to Its Proper Height; Forget Burying the Infamous Roadway. The Solution to Waterfront Woes May Lie in Celebrating the Space Beneath." *Globe and Mail*, 17 November.

Campion-Smith, Bruce. 1994. "New Rules May Cut Island Airport Fire Hall." *Toronto Star*, 23 August.

Caulfield, Jon. 1974. *The Tiny Perfect Mayor*. Toronto: Lorimer.

Cervero, R., and M. Duncan. 2006. "Which Reduces Vehicle Travel More: Jobs-Housing Balance or Retail-Housing Mixture?" *Journal of the American Planning Association* 72: 475–90.

City of Toronto Planning and Development Department. 1993. *City of Toronto Official Plan: Part I – CityPlan: By-law 423-93*. Toronto: City of Toronto, Department of Planning and Development.

City of Toronto Planning Board. 1950. *Third Report and Official Plan*. Toronto: City of Toronto Planning Board.

– 1963. *Plan for Downtown Toronto: A Report*. Toronto: City of Toronto Planning Board.

– 1974. *The Central Waterfront: Proposal for Planning*. Toronto: City of Toronto Planning Board.

City of Toronto Planning & Development Department. 1991. *Cityplan '91: Proposals Report – June 1991*. Toronto: City of Toronto Planning & Development Department.

Clarke, Susan E. 1995. "Institutional Logics and Local Economic Development: A Comparative Analysis of Eight American Cities." *International Journal of Urban and Regional Research* 19: 513–33.

Community AIR. 2007. http://communityair.org/.

Dalby, Paul. 1980. "Cosgrove Wooing MPs on New Harbourfront Plan." *Toronto Star*, 15 May.

DeMara, Bruce. 1999. "The Concrete Divide." *Toronto Star*, 7 August.

Desfor, Gene. 1993. "Restructuring the Toronto Harbour Commission: Land Politics on the Toronto Waterfront." *Journal of Transport Geography* 1, no. 3: 167–81.

Desfor, Gene, Michael Goldrick, and Roy Merrens. 1989. "A Political Economy of the Water-Frontier: Planning and Development in Toronto." *Geoforum* 20, no. 4: 487–501.

Dineen, J. 1979. "Liberals' Fall Leaves Harbourfront in Limbo." *Toronto Star*, 7 October.

Donald, B. 2002. "Spinning Toronto's Golden Age: The Making of a 'City that Worked.'" *Environment and Planning A* 34: 2127–54.

Dutton, D. 1969. "Only Luxury Apartments Feasible in Harbor Study." *Toronto Star*, 10 April.

Filion, Pierre. 2001. "The Urban Policy-Making and Development Dimension of Fordism and Post-Fordism: A Toronto Case Study." *Space and Polity* 52, no. 2: 85–111.

Fine, S. 1986. "Taxpayers May Be the Losers in Land Sale, Councillors Fear." *Globe and Mail*, 30 August.

Frank, Lawrence D., Sarah Kavage, and Bruce Appleyard. 2007. "The Urban Form and Climate Change." *Urban Planning* 73, no. 8: 18–23.

Fraser, G. 1976. "Harbourfront Is not Dead – It's Just Sleeping." *Globe and Mail*, 25 May.

Gans, Herbert J. 1962. *The Urban Villagers: Group and Class in the Life of Italian Americans*. New York: Free Press of Glencoe.

Gibbon, A. 1997. "Terry Hui's Real Estate Star Poised to Rise to New Level." *Globe and Mail*, 10 July.

Gillespie, Kerry. 2004a. "Fung Weary of Playing Waterfront Games; Corporation Head Upset about Slow Pace of Development; Lack of Funds, Bureaucracy Described as Major Hurdles." *Toronto Star*, 4 March.

– 2004b. "Waterfront Corporation Starved for Cash, May Fold; Said to Be 26 days from Shutdown; Projects Delayed; Ottawa Owes $10M." *Toronto Star*, 5 March.

– 2006. "From 'Wasted' to 'People' Place. West Don Lands Development Just Makes Sense, Caplan Says." *Toronto Star*, 27 March.

Globe and Mail. 1963a. "Board of Control Approves Waterfront Plan." 27 July.

– 1963b. "Waterfront Project Backed." 17 October.

– 1965. "City, Developer Sign Deal on Waterfront." 4 September.

– 1979. "Harbourfront Gets Pledge of Financing." 31 March.

– 1980a. "Harborfront Plan Placates Opponents." 14 June.

– 1980b. "Toronto Lays Groundwork for Waterfront Community." 24 June.

Goldrick, M., and R. Merrens. 1990. "Waterfront Changes and Institutional States: The Role of the Toronto Harbour Commission, 1911–1989." In *Port Cities in Context: The Impact of Waterfront Regeneration*, edited by B.S. Hoyle. Southhampton UK: Institute of British Geographers, 119–153.

Gonda, Gabe. 2006. "Air Canada Loses Island Airport Fight." *Toronto Star*, 28 February.

Gooderman, M. 1986. "Harbourfront Apartments Approved over Accusations of Rushing Project." *Globe and Mail*, 23 April.

Gordon, David L.A. 1994. "Implementing Urban Waterfront Redevelopment." PhD diss. Cambridge MA: Harvard University.

Government of Canada. 1911. Statutes, Act 1–2 George V, Chapter 26. Ottawa: Government of Canada.

– 1996. Bill C-44, *The Canada Marine Act*. Ottawa: Government of Canada.

Government of Canada and Nielsen Task Force on Program Review. 1985. "Real Property." In *Report of the Nielsen Task Force on Program Review*. Ottawa: Ministry of Supply and Services.

Government of Ontario. 2002. Toronto Waterfront Revitalization Corporation Act, 2002, S.O. 2002, Chapter 28.

Greenberg, K. 1996. "Toronto: The Urban Waterfront as a Terrain of Availability." In *City, Capital and Water*, edited by P. Malone. London and New York: Routledge, 195–218.

Harbourfront Corporation. 1978. *Harbourfront Development Framework*. Toronto: Harbourfront Corporation.

Harding, K. 2004. "Mayor Urges Ottawa to Sign Deal Killing Bridge." *Globe and Mail*, 13 May.

Hartmann, Franz. 1999. "Nature in the City: Urban Ecological Politics in Toronto." PhD diss. Toronto: York University.

Hodge, G. 1972. "The Care and Feeding of an Airport, or the Technocrat as Midwife." In *The City: Attacking Modern Myths*, edited by A. Powell. Toronto: McLelland & Stewart, 210–19.

Hume, Christopher. 2002a. "Fung's Waterfront Revitalization Group on the Way to Become a Paper Tiger." *Toronto Star*, 25 Sepember.

– 2002b. "Waterfront Corporation Still Adrift with No Power." *Toronto Star*, 9 May.

– 2004. "Going Madly Off in All Directions." *Toronto Star*, 7 October.

– 2007. "New Designs Must Impress; Group Pulls Funding, Says Best Parts of Building Plans Gone." *Toronto Star*, 8 December.

Ircha, Michael C. 1993. "Institutional Structure of Canadian Ports." *Maritime Policy and Management* 20, no. 1: 51–66.

Jabereen, Yosef R. 2006. "Sustainable Urban Forms: Their Typologies, Models, and Concepts." *Journal of Planning Education and Research* 26: 38–52.

Jacobs, Jane. 1961. *The Death and Life of Great American Cities*. New York: Random House.

James, Royson. 2000a. "Land 'Scandal' Spoils Task Force's Big Day." *Toronto Star*, 27 March.

– 2000b. "TEDCO Fumble Could Trip Up Fung's Plan." *Toronto Star*, 17 April.

– 2001. "Waterfront's Future Stuck in Limbo – Report's Ready, but Lastman's Support Isn't." *Toronto Star*, 26 September.

Kashmeri, Z. 1986. "City, Harbourfront Agree on Plan for Limited Waterfront Development." *Globe and Mail*, 8 April.

Kenworthy, Jeffrey R. 2006. "The Eco-City: Ten Key Transport and Planning Dimensions for Sustainable City Development." *Environment and Urbanization* 18: 67–85.

Kerr, T. 1986a. "$24 Million Sale of Harbor Land Called Too Low." *Toronto Star*, 28 August.

– 1986b. "Harbor Commission Refuses Demand for Land Sale Details." *Toronto Star*, 20 August.

Kipfer, Stefan, and Roger Keil 2002. "Toronto Inc? Planning the Competitive City in the New Toronto." *Antipode* 34, no. 2: 227–64.

Kumar, Krishan. 1995. *From Post-Industrialism to Post-Modern Society: New Theories for the Contemporary World*. Oxford UK: Blackwell.

Laidley, Jennifer. 2007. "The Ecosystem Approach and the Global Imperative on Toronto's Central Waterfront." *Cities* 24, no. 4: 251–334.

Lakey, J. 2000. "Waterfront Chief Warned Against Deals – Port-Land Officials Went Ahead with 20-Year Lease." *Toronto Star*, 27 March.

– 2001. "Superagency to Redevelop Waterfront – Three Governments Kick In $300 Million to Start Key Projects." *Toronto Star*, 1 March.

Lakey, Jack, and Boris Spremo. 2000. "Mystery as Tycoon Steve Stavro Wins New 20-Year Lease." *Toronto Star*, 25 March.

Laver, R. 1981. "Office Tower Is Proposed for Waterfront." *Globe and Mail*, 10 December.

Lecours, Andre, ed. 2005. *New Institutionalism: Theory and Analysis*. Toronto: University of Toronto Press.

Lemon, James. 1990. *The Toronto Harbour Plan of 1912: Manufacturing Goals and Economic Realities*. Toronto: Canadian Waterfront Resource Centre.

Lewington, Jennifer. 2004. "Waterfront Renewal Hits Snag; Public Agency Wants More Authority to Deal with Chronic Cash-Flow Problems." *Globe and Mail*, 8 March.

– 2005a. "Ottawa Pays $35-Million to Abort Bridge." *Globe and Mail*, 4 May.

– 2005b. "West Don Lands Get the Nod." *Globe and Mail*, 6 May.

Macaulay, R. 1992. *Report on the Toronto Harbour Commission and Recommendations for the Future*. Toronto: Waterfront Regeneration Trust.

March, James G., and Johan P. Olsen. 1984. *Rediscovering Institutions*. New York: Free Press.

Mariport Group Ltd. 1999. *Evaluating the Port of Toronto: Markets and Impacts on the GTA*. Toronto: Mariport Group Ltd.

Mays, J.B. 2004. "A Kinder, Gentler Queens Quay; Waterclub's Buxom Towers Have Created a Comforting Closeness at Street Level." *Globe and Mail*, 3 December.

Mclaughlin, David J. 1992. "The Planning and Development of Harbourfront: An Historical Analysis." MA thesis. Toronto: York University.

McLaughlin, S. 1987. *Federal Land Management in the Toronto Region*. Toronto: Stephen G. McLaughlin Consultants.

Mellen, Frances. 1974. "The Development of the Toronto Waterfront During the Railway Expansion Era, 1850–1912." PhD diss. Toronto: University of Toronto.

Merrens, Roy. 1988. "Port Authorities as Urban Land Developers: The Case of the Toronto Harbour Commissioners and Their Outer Harbour Project, 1912–68." *Urban History Review* 17, no. 2: 92–105.

Metropolitan Toronto Planning Board. 1967. *The Waterfront Plan for the Metropolitan Toronto Planning Area*. Toronto: Metropolitan Toronto Planning Board.

– 1970. *Metro Centre: A Review of the Proposed Development on the Canadian National and Canadian Pacific Railway Lands in Downtown Toronto*. Toronto: Metropolitan Toronto Planning Board.

Miller, D. 1979. "Shops and Housing – That's the Plan for Harbourfront." *Toronto Star*, 9 February.

Miron, John R., ed. 1993. *House, Home and Community: Progress in Housing Canadians, 1945–1986*. Montreal & Kingston: McGill-Queen's University Press.

Moloney, P. 1996. "City Balks at Ottawa's Port Plan; Won't Give Up Control to Business Board." *Toronto Star*, 29 March.

– 2002. "Island Airport Fans Reject Passenger Limit – 'It Could Kill the Deal,' Meeting Told." *Toronto Star*, 25 October.

Monsebraaten, Laurie. 1987. "Aldermen to Replace Citizens on Harbour Commission; Toronto Seeks More Waterfront Control." *Toronto Star*, 16 June.

Palango, Paul. 1979. "Yonge Street the Great Dividing Line as PCs, Liberals Split 22 Metro Ridings." *Globe and Mail*, 23 May.

Perloff, Harvey S. 1980. *Planning the Post-Industrial City*. Chicago: Planners Press.

Pooley, Erin, and Katherine Harding. 2003. "Bridge to Airport Receives a Quiet Nod from Ottawa." *Globe and Mail*, 4 November.

Province of Ontario Department of Trade & Development. 1970. *A New Illustrated Concept for the Harbour City Development by the Government of Ontario*. Toronto: Province of Ontario Department of Trade & Development.

Radkewycz, Alexandra. 1986. "Chief Planner for Toronto Steps Down." *Globe and Mail*, 20 October.

Ramlalsingh, Roderick D. 1975. *A Study of the Decline of Trade at the Port of Toronto*. Toronto: York University Department of Geography Discussion Paper Series.

Rickwood, P., and H. Mietkiewicz. 1980. "Ottawa Gives Harbourfront $25 Million." *Toronto Star*, 13 June.

Royal Commission on the Future of the Toronto Waterfront. 1989a. *Interim Report: Summer, 1989*. Toronto: Royal Commission on the Future of the Toronto Waterfront.

– 1989b. *Persistence and Change: Waterfront Issues and the Board of Toronto Harbour Commissioners*. Toronto: Royal Commission on the Future of the Toronto Waterfront.

– 1990. *Watershed*. Toronto: Royal Commission on the Future of the Toronto Waterfront.

– 1991. *Regeneration: Toronto's Waterfront and the Sustainable City: Final Report*. Toronto: Royal Commission on the Future of the Toronto Waterfront.

Rusk, J. 1999. "City Waterfront to Be 'Magic Place' in Redevelopment." *Globe and Mail*, 4 November.

– 2001. "Fung Enthused by Nomination to Head Waterfront Agency." *Globe and Mail*, 5 July.

– 2002. "Crombie, Jacobs Attack Airport Plan." *Globe and Mail*, 26 November.

Safieddine, Hicham, and Royson James. 2005. "Bridge Battle Finally Over." *Toronto Star*, 4 May.

Savitch, H.V. 1988. *Post-Industrial Cities: Politics and Planning in New York, Paris and London*. Princeton NJ: Princeton University Press.

Schaeffer, Roy. 1974. *The Board of Trade and the Origins of the Toronto Harbour Commissioners, 1899–1911*. Toronto: York University Department of Geography Discussion Paper Series.

Sewell, John. 1972. *Up Against City Hall*. Toronto: James Lorimer.

Stein, David Lewis. 1979. "Good Guys Sound like Bad Guys." *Toronto Star*, 9 December.

– 1987. "Parks Commissioner vs. Harbourfront." *Toronto Star*, 2 January.

Tassé, Roger. 2006. *Review of Toronto Port Authority Report*. Toronto: Gowling Lafleur Henderson LLP Barristers & Solicitors.

Taylor, P. 1986. "Council Approves $400 Million Waterfront Development." *Globe and Mail*, 2 December.

– 1987. "Direction of Harbourfront Assailed by Residents." *Globe and Mail*, 18 March.

Toronto City Council. 1982. *Agreement Between Harbourfront Corporation and the Corporation of the City of Toronto, December 1982*. Toronto: Toronto City Council.

Toronto Harbour Commissioners. 1912. *Toronto Waterfront Development, 1912–1920*. Toronto: Toronto Harbour Commissioners.

Toronto Harbour Commission. 1968. *A Bold Concept for the Redevelopment of the Toronto Waterfront*. Toronto: Toronto Harbour Commission.

Toronto Planning Board. 1962. *The Core of the Central Waterfront: A Proposal by the City of Toronto Planning Board*. Toronto: Toronto Planning Board.

– 1977a. *Central Area Plan*. Toronto: Toronto Planning Board.

– 1977b. *Official Plan for the City of Toronto Planning Area as Amended and Approved – Part I – Office Consolidation*. Toronto: Toronto Planning Board.

Toronto Planning Department. 1980. *Harbourfront Part 2 Official Plan (Office Consolidation)*. Toronto: Toronto Planning Department.

Toronto Waterfront Revitalization Corporation. 2005. *Commissioners Park*. Toronto: TWRC.

Toronto Waterfront Revitalization Task Force. 2000. *Our Toronto Waterfront: Building Momentum*. Toronto: TWRTF.

Walkom, T. 2003. "Bridge over Troubled Waters." *Toronto Star*, 14 October.

Wanagas, Don. 2002. "Councillors Have Killed Waterfront: Airport Expansion, Bridge Approved Despite Concerns." *National Post*, 29 November.

Welsh, M., and Jack Lakey. 2001. "Waterfront Agency Raises Concerns – Accountability of Unelected Board Questioned." *Toronto Star*, 2 March.

Wolfe, Jeanne M. 2003. "A National Urban Policy for Canada? Prospects and Challenges." *Canadian Journal of Urban Research* 12, no. 1: 1–21.

Wong, T. 1997. "$2 Billion Plan Will Transform Railway Land." *Toronto Star*, 26 March.

– 2003. "Trizec to Unload Stake in CN Tower; Original Landlord Canada Lands to Manage Landmark; Deal Valued at an Estimated $35 Million U.S." *Toronto Star*, 26 March.

Zehr, L. 1996. "12 Firms Vie to Revamp Toronto Railway Lands; Crown Corporation Seeks Proposals to Turn Derelict Property into Entertainment Complex." *Globe and Mail*, 13 September.

– 1997. "Grand Design for Toronto's Railway Lands Faces Hearing; Vancouver Developer's $1 Billion Plan Would Revamp City's Skyline." *Globe and Mail*, 24 September.

6

Conclusion

MICHAEL C. IRCHA AND ROBERT YOUNG

Property owned by the federal government is scattered across Canada from coast to coast to coast. In a myriad of ways, these lands, buildings, and installations affect every Canadian resident. In a more sustained and direct fashion, federal property affects the municipalities it lies within or near, and in some instances policies about property are not only important to citizens and municipal governments but are also vital to the socio-economic evolution of the whole community. The chapters collected here have explored many instances where decisions about federal property have been significant at the municipal level. To take up the terms used in the chapter by Summerville, Wilson, and Young, we can distinguish between perennial and dynamic issues in the field of federal property. The former affect all municipalities. Dynamic issues involve high-visibility federal property that is undergoing substantial change – airports, ports, parks, and military bases in particular – in individual communities, and these are the focus of most of the research presented in this volume.

Our studies have revealed many dimensions of policy-making in the field of federal property. In this Conclusion we will analyze them, first searching for common patterns and also for differences, then bringing the rich case material to bear on general questions of theoretical interest, and finally assessing the quality of policy in the field with the intent of suggesting improvements. In the course of this discussion we will explore two aspects of the field that distinguish it from most other areas of government policy. First, in many of the dynamic issues it is evident that policies determine politics, in a clear and predictable manner. Second, in most instances a precise value can be placed on property. The transparency of this value (or lack thereof) places unusual pressure on policy-makers and shapes policy outputs in a fundamental way. The politics of dynamic property issues are often difficult – more tumultuous and conflict-ridden than they need to be. We think that the policy process would be less acrimonious and more efficient if a new agency were made responsible for coordinating federal property management insofar as it involves municipalities.

The research collected here breaks new ground. In the scholarly literature, there is no coherent work focused on government property in Canada that is set within the preoccupations of political science and public administration, and that explores the policy-making process in a sustained and comparative fashion. The authors of the studies collected here have explored property issues in twelve municipalities, in depth. They have used documentary materials, newspaper accounts, and secondary literature. They also conducted thirty-eight interviews with officials, politicians, and representatives of various organized interests ("social forces," in our terms). This thoroughness is unprecedented. There is also good geographical coverage. We selected four provinces for the federal property studies, and we believe that they are representative of the situation in Canada as a whole. British Columbia is something of an outlier because First Nations' land claims are very much unsettled there, and this complicates all property issues. But there are outstanding Aboriginal land claims in many other parts of the country too. There are no Prairie provinces included here, but the introductory chapter provided a national overview of federal-municipal property issues that explored some in Manitoba and elsewhere, and we have no reason to think that patterns found in our research are not characteristic of other provinces as well. Finally, as part of the larger project of which this volume is a component, studies were done of federal property issues in several large Canadian cities, and results there were similar to those found in the work reported here.[1]

PERENNIAL ISSUES

Federal property brings many benefits to municipal governments and residents. Properties normally house public servants, and their jobs are well paid, particularly in comparison to most workers' wages in peripheral communities. These payrolls are important for local businesses in the retail and service sectors. Many other local firms benefit as suppliers of goods and services to federal installations of various kinds. All these incomes are sources of provincial tax revenues, while municipal governments benefit from the tax base provided by residential and commercial development linked to federal facilities, and by the properties themselves (which do not pay municipal taxes per se but provide payments in lieu of taxes, or PILTs). These are simple reasons for municipal (and provincial) governments to be interested in federal property, and in smaller municipalities where federal activities can dominate local economies a continued federal presence can be seen as essential to the viability of the community.

There are perennial issues about federal property that concern municipal governments. One is the level of PILT. These payments are meant to compensate municipalities for the services they provide to federal property – fire protection, policing, snow removal, and so on. In many cases, municipal governments perceive that PILTs do not cover the full cost of the services provided. Even more commonly, PILTs do not amount to the property taxes that would be collected were federal property assessed and taxed like other lands and buildings. It is sometimes difficult to assess the value of federal holdings such as ports and military bases, and this is typically not attempted by municipal and provincial property assessors. But in the city of Ottawa, for example, there appears to be a considerable gap between PILTs and the amount of property taxes that would be paid, based on the property values set by the Ontario Municipal Assessment Corporation (Adam 2010). Municipal governments are irritated by such discrepancies and frustrated by the federal government's unilateralism in setting PILT levels.

Another significant issue that perennially disturbs federal-municipal relations concerns local by-laws. Due to their constitutional status, federal lands lie outside municipal jurisdiction with respect to local planning, zoning, and building by-laws and regulations. This problem bedevils the handling of land in urban settings, as it did at Downsview Park in Toronto, when the federal agency responsible for the property's development insisted on its paramountcy and did not submit to the municipal planning process. It took a city resolution – and a change of the agency's board of directors – to bring about Downsview Park's submission to the municipal planning authority (Horak 2012, 140). Overall, it appears that some federal agencies and departments abide by local regulations, while others choose not to do so.

Two other related issues arise with much federal property. One is the extent to which federal authorities are prepared to spend to maintain properties and to invest in them. As the case study of Placentia shows, this can be a serious source of concern to municipal governments. Related to this are the linkages between federal property and associated infrastructure that may need to be provided by municipal or provincial authorities. The latter may be required to build and maintain roads and other facilities to support federal installations. The Newfoundland chapter illustrates the conflicts that may arise because of these expenditure needs.

Perennial issues about federal property are not often matters of much public interest. They often involve rather technical questions, and are normally handled by officials rather than politicians. Few actors are involved. Normally, municipal representatives have little influence in such negotiations as may take place: the federal departments and agencies typically receive communities' representations, but decision-making lies in Ottawa's hands. Municipal frustration is sometimes expressed by provincial associations of municipalities and by the Federation of Canadian Municipalities, but still the federal government predominates.

DYNAMIC ISSUES

Most of the cases presented in this book focus on dynamic issues. In these cases, major decisions are taken about federal property. There are some instances of new acquisitions of land by the federal government. But these are rare in the contemporary period; moreover, they seem to be handled smoothly, to the mutual satisfaction of the parties concerned. Divestitures are different. As many cases in this volume demonstrate, the closure of military bases and the transfer of control of airports and ports are explosive issues. The principles of New Public Management underlie divestitures. But these are highly politicized and engender a lot of public mobilization. Divestitures may in fact represent instances in which "policies determine politics."

This phrase originates with the distinguished political scientist Theodore Lowi (1972, 299; 1964). His underlying notion is that the nature of the policy that is on the table shapes the patterns of politics that arise around it. For example, redistributive policies generate ideological disputes involving large interest groups which are very stable and have professional expertise, distributive policies generate logrolling by politicians, and so on. Lowi's work is ingenious and much cited, but the core schema has been little used. This is probably because there are political processes behind agenda-setting, problem definition, and the movement of policy ideas into various policy arenas. In the view of most, therefore, politics determines what policies get onto the table and how they are framed, and so the policy does not really engender the subsequent politics.

Dynamic federal property issues, however, may approximate the Lowi mechanism. This is because the federal government often makes unexpected policy announcements, and these produce a clear pattern of politics that is widely evident. The politics begin with the shock of the announcement. The Chilliwack base closure provides an example. Notice of the decision came as a clear surprise; the politics followed. It is true that closures can be anticipated and resisted in advance. Moncton fought the potential closure of the CN Shops for twenty years, and the Happy Valley–Goose Bay community mobilized around a base closure that seems to have taken place in slow motion. The Chatham base closure was feared and fought for a long time.

But when the announcement comes, it is a galvanizing shock. Resistance is quickly mobilized. Here, municipal politicians and the business community take a leading role. In Fredericton, for instance, both local politicians and businesspeople were very much opposed to plans to divest the airport, and they were vocal. In Happy Valley–Goose Bay, the chamber of commerce strongly resisted the base closure. Next, under this leadership, citizens are mobilized into a broad coalition to oppose the policy. This was seen in Chilliwack; in Chatham, over 7,000 people marched in protest. Other organizations such as unions participate in these coalitions.

The pressure is highly political. It is often led by the mayor. People in the office of mayor are normally just equal in voting power to other members of local councils, but the mayor is the face of the municipality, and a big part of her or his duties consists of external relations. Hence the mayor generally leads the resistance to property changes that threaten the community. Neighbouring municipalities are also enlisted, as in the Fredericton and Prince George airport examples. The local coalition leaders work through political channels. They prevail upon and often enlist local members of Parliament, and they appeal to the regional minister. Pressure is also applied to provincial politicians and their support is solicited. In the case of the Prince George airport divestiture and negotiations, for example, the province placed its weight – and money – behind the municipal authorities, and this is typical. The government of Newfoundland and Labrador seems to have been more reluctant than most to support the municipalities, largely in fear of taking on financial commitments, but in the Chatham case, the province of New Brunswick was heavily involved, with even the premier intervening. In Chilliwack, the British Columbia government helped to lever a plan for mitigation and renewal.

This is the next phase. If the decision is irrevocable, then local attention turns toward the future. Generally the business community organizes new thinking about potential economic development – alternative ownership models for airports and ports, different uses for base property, and new activities to substitute for the military. The Chatham plans were contrived by local business leaders, and business spearheads the Goose Bay Airport Corporation. Other local institutions are also involved, as was the College of the Fraser Valley in Chilliwack. In these planning efforts, local and provincial interests press for federal assistance. This can take several forms. There are demands that Ottawa make further investment in facilities in order to remediate them or to make them more viable before a divestment, as at the Fredericton airport. The government is also pressed to prolong the transition, and to provide financial assistance for new initiatives, as in the Chilliwack case, where determined pressure and a well-developed business case drew the federal government into planning for redevelopment. Sometimes support for investment can be leveraged from the regional economic development agencies – the Atlantic Canada Opportunities Agency and Western Economic Diversification Canada. Finally, very strong pressure can elicit replacement activities by the federal government itself. The Central Processing Site for the Canadian firearms registry was established in Miramichi, New Brunswick (into which Chatham was merged after the base closure). And when the base in Summerside PEI was closed in 1989, a partial substitute was found in the form of the processing centre for the Goods and Services Tax (Savoie 1995).

These dynamic issues can cause substantial economic disruption and political perturbation. On the political side, base closures especially create huge transaction costs – the time, energy, and resources devoted to resistance, lobbying, and negotiations. It is not just the decision itself that produces these effects, but also the shock of sudden and surprising announcements. In recent years, the systematic and relatively transparent process that is used in the United States to handle base closures has been far superior, politically, to its Canadian counterpart (Goren and Lackenbauer 2003). Briefly, the key US actor is the Base Realignment and Closing Commission (BRAC). This independent commission receives recommendations, in the form of a list of possible closures, from the military, through the Secretary of Defense. BRAC analyzes data and holds public hearings, and prepares a final list for the president, who can submit it to Congress, where individual amendments or deletions are not permitted. This insulates the process from partisan politics and removes a good deal of surprise and uncertainty, while being fairly transparent.

One can argue that Canada needs a more transparent decision-making process, one that also takes socio-economic factors into account from the outset. Into the closure decision should be incorporated transition plans and compensatory investments, ones that reflect the economic conditions of the community. Closures in peripheral, isolated communities such as Chatham are much more wrenching than in centres such as Winnipeg, and this fact needs to be considered from the beginning (Savoie 1995, 70–5). In the end, as our cases of divestiture and closure show, the inevitable resistance and political pressure is generally powerful enough to induce federal investments that moderate the blow of the initial federal policy. When threatened, municipalities, with some assistance, are eventually capable of generating new opportunities. But the normal policy process in dynamic federal property transfers results in highly dysfunctional politics and difficult transitions. There must be a way to avoid these costs and to accelerate progress toward a satisfactory result.

GENERAL CONSIDERATIONS

Now we take up the general issues that are illuminated by the cases explored here. These are also relevant to other policy fields where multilevel governance (MLG) is found. The first set of issues concerns intergovernmental relations – the multilevel part of MLG – and the first of these is simply to analyze the kinds of linkages that exist between municipal and federal authorities. In the field of federal property, these relations generally are very tenuous. There is rarely an interlocutor at the federal level that is open to municipal contacts and familiar with municipal issues. As a consequence, municipalities are reduced to sending delegations to Ottawa, presenting their cases to officials in various departments. This was done notably by Chilliwack and Saint John (with respect to the harbour). Interviews with respondents from the municipal level consistently depicted how difficult relations can be with federal officials. The Department of National Defence was particularly impervious to the entreaties of representatives from Chatham and from Happy Valley–Goose Bay. With few exceptions, mechanisms for continuous interaction between municipal governments and federal departments and agencies do not exist, and trust and mutual understanding are weak. Disagreement and frustration are common.

Municipalities' relationships with Ottawa, such as they are, generally are bolstered by provincial governments. Provincial politicians, sometimes supported by expert officials, normally sustain and amplify the municipal positions. Politicians at the provincial level were heavily involved in resistance to base closures and in subsequent negotiations about replacement activities. (A partial exception was the government of Newfoundland and Labrador, which has been hesitant to fully engage in issues about federal property.) So the provinces are helpful in bilateral relations.[2] In cases where they perceive a strong provincial interest, and become involved as direct actors, however, provincial governments can be more problematic for municipalities. As the Toronto waterfront case amply shows, three-player games can become very complicated. Difficult negotiations, delay, and unmet expectations are often the result of tripartite relationships. In any event, it is perfectly clear that the shape of public policy about federal property is strongly determined by intergovernmental relations.

In dynamic federal property issues, politicians come to the fore. The Moncton case provides a good example of local politicians working with members of Parliament and the federal minister responsible for the province. Mayors can make a real difference. In Toronto, strong mayors such as David Crombie and David Miller did influence the decisions that the federal government made about waterfront issues. The latter, for instance, was able to convince Ottawa to abandon the proposed bridge link to the Toronto Island Airport, despite previous city council approvals and a signed construction contract.

Individual provincial ministers can also make a difference when they are active on a property file. And federal politicians and ministers are also important. For example, the minister of National Defence (and Toronto MP) David Collenette intervened in the redevelopment of the former Downsview Airport site by promising that it would become a park. And at the apex of federal politics, Prime Ministers Mulroney and Chrétien both took an interest in the Chatham air base. In most policy fields involving municipal interests, most of the time, it is officials rather than politicians who take charge. Dynamic issues involving federal property constitute a striking exception.

Given the involvement of politicians in the federal property field, it is not surprising that ideology plays some role in policy-making. This is evident in several interventions about the Toronto waterfront that occurred when the ideological balance of power on city council shifted from right to left and vice-versa. It is also apparent in British Columbia, where the provincial Liberals were more inclined to collaborate with federal politicians than was the preceding New Democratic government. And yet personal relationships and individual preferences seem to matter more than political ideology in this policy field. Intergovernmental relations are often very personal, as the New Brunswick cases show. Personal links were also important during the long saga of Happy Valley–Goose Bay and its base. On the Toronto waterfront, the personal proclivities of politicians have been crucial in producing policy shifts – the new orientation of Premier Bill Davis, the support of the Mulroney government for subsidized housing, the development freeze, the determination of Toronto MPs to maintain a federal presence, and so on. This historical case study is most instructive in showing the importance of political and personal factors in making policy about federal property.

Another general issue concerns the balance of resources between the governments engaged in policy-making. In this policy field, municipal governments are in a very weak bargaining position relative to Ottawa. However, they are not powerless by any means. Their leverage seems to depend on their size and on the relative importance of the federal property in the community. Some municipalities also have technical expertise that is often lacking in other levels of government. The power of professional planners was evident in Toronto, both at Downsview Park and on the waterfront, though planning expertise was only one element in the mix of resources deployed. But generally municipal governments are policy takers. In this field they neither set the agenda nor determine policy outcomes, because they have few resources. For the most part they cannot sustain lengthy and technical lobbying of federal officials in Ottawa, either financially or analytically. In this policy area, municipal weakness is compounded by the fact that local issues about federal property are, in most cases, unique. This means that municipal governments cannot rely on the expertise and political clout of the collective organizations representing municipalities, at either the federal or the provincial level. The Federation of Canadian Municipalities and the provincial associations are much more effective where perennial issues are concerned than when the federal government is making new dynamic policy about particular facilities. Provincial governments, however, can strengthen the bargaining power of municipal governments. As the Chilliwack and Chatham cases demonstrate, a determined municipal-provincial coalition can extract substantial benefits from the federal government. At other times Ottawa simply seems inclined to share resources. For example, most municipal services at Argentia are federally funded through the Argentia Management Authority; similarly, the Canada Lands Company undertook a generous remediation program in Moncton. These cases may simply illustrate the discretion – the power – that the federal government enjoys in matters concerning its property.

The final general issue in intergovernmental relations concerns New Public Management (NPM), and its effects on the policy process. Some core elements of NPM were sketched in the Introduction – improved efficiency, cost recovery, privatization, delegation to specialized agencies as well as private and non-profit organizations, more latitude for public servants, and a general orientation toward having government shape policy rather than delivering it; that is, "steering" rather than "rowing."[3] The shift towards NPM principles in the 1980s and 1990s has probably had a greater impact on property management than on any other area of federal activity. In 1984, the Task Force on Program Review headed by Erik Nielsen began to conduct a sweeping assessment of government operations and programs. An important component of this was to rethink federal property management and to complete an inventory of federal holdings (Canada 1986). This was followed by the Federal Real Property Act of 1992, which simplified and modernized the management of property. A real impetus to change was the fiscal crisis that faced the government led by Jean Chrétien in 1994. Its very substantial deficits forced Ottawa to cut back federal operations and expenditures. There was a strongly perceived need to do things differently. From this flowed the creation of the Canada Port Authorities, the divestiture of airports under the National Airport Policy, and the reduction of military bases, stations, and detachments from fifty-two in 1994 to twenty-four in 2000 (Goren and Lackenbauer 2003, 192 note 87). New Public Management provides the backdrop to most of the dynamic cases examined in this book.

Another feature of New Public Management is the creation of specialized agencies that can act more nimbly than traditional bureaucracies. In 1995 the federal government revived the Canada Lands Company (CLC).[4] This agency was to assist federal departments and Crown corporations to dispose of their surplus property and so to generate revenue for the federal government. At the time, the CLC's core mandate was "to optimize the value gained from the management or development and orderly disposal of [federal] lands on behalf of the people of Canada" (Canada Lands Company 1999, 4). Between 1995 and 1998 the CLC generated $147 million for the federal government, and by 2009 the net return from CLC activities over a fourteen-year period had reached $373 million (Canada Lands Company 2010, 2). The CLC is market-oriented in a way that exemplifies NPM principles. It acquires surplus federal lands from departments and agencies at market value, and then it develops and revitalizes these properties before re-integrating them into the local community. The CLC adds value to the divested federal lands by retaining, managing, and improving the assets or by developing and selling the lands to generate maximum financial returns. Among the cases studied here, there are instances where the CLC was driven by political pressure to depart from the core objective of maximization; that is, instances where market principles and considerations of business risk were overridden. This was true in Moncton, where one participant in redeveloping the CN Shops lands described the process simply: "there was no business case for what we did." Normally, however, the CLC and other actors are constrained by market forces, and more precisely by the value of the federal property at issue. We will return to this feature of the policy field shortly.

Our second set of general questions concerns social forces and the role that they play in the policy process. This is the governance part of MLG. The first issue here is which local groups have been involved. Across the cases, there is a lot of variation in this regard. In the instances of military base closures, very broad coalitions formed at the local level, uniting all groups in the community. These were normally led by local business interests, and business took the lead again when new plans and alternatives had to be formulated. At that point, other interests often tended to mute their criticism, because the whole community now depended on new development taking place, as was seen in Prince Rupert in particular. In other divestitures such as airports, participation was narrower, mostly confined to business interests. In British Columbia, First Nations have been important actors in every dynamic issue. As Summerville, Wilson, and Young explain, they participate both as social forces, expressing demands like other groups, and as governments, given their unique constitutional status. In property issues, First Nations often have a strong bargaining position – and not just in British Columbia. The greatest number and diversity of social forces were found in the Toronto waterfront case, which attracted the participation of residents' groups, housing advocates, heritage-preservation interests, boaters, environmentalists, loose coalitions of urban reformers, and, of course, business interests. The last were mainly developers, but, as in the Saint John harbour case, other businesses had an interest in protecting the rights of shippers and established industries operating on the waterfront. In any event, our expectations about the important role of social forces in policy-making about federal property are clearly upheld.

What interests predominate in policy about federal property? In general, it is business. In the airport divestitures, for example, local businesses led efforts to install viable management and financial structures. Municipal politicians and officials may have conducted negotiations, but business interests set the agenda and forced the pace. Often, this leadership is uncontested. Businesses have a large stake in the economic viability of their communities, many property issues are technical or involve financial matters that are arcane to most citizens, and maintaining ports and airports and redeveloping bases can be seen as benefitting the whole community. So weak opposition or no opposition to a business consensus characterized many of our cases. Indeed, in some extreme instances such as the Waterfront Development Partnership in Saint John, local businesses played a direct role in planning and development.

But business interests are not always unchallenged or successful. The perceived interests of First Nations may prevail, because of their special rights that are enforced by courts, not through the political process. Neighbourhood groups can help shape plans for parks, and a group in Toronto's Beaches community managed to stop an airport. Heritage groups and civic activists saved Union Station. Perhaps most significantly, in battles over Harbourfront, the Toronto Board of Trade found itself on the losing side of important issues. Non-business interests seem to prevail under certain conditions. Broad and intense public mobilization can score victories, or at least force some compromises. Citizens' groups and environmental and heritage interests can receive support from planners, a strong bulwark of professional expertise in the big cities. Finally, business can be divided, as is especially apparent in struggles over port lands. Firms in sectors such as tourism and the service industries can be the allies of environmentalists in conflicts with heavy industry, shipping, and other sectors.

In multilevel governance, we are concerned not only with what interests are involved and which are successful but also with the capacity of groups to be effective at other scales than the local. Can local interests influence policy at the provincial and federal levels? From our research, the answer is mixed. Local interests of all kinds have a difficult time dealing with the federal bureaucracy, more so even than municipal governments. Sometimes local social forces can operate through members of Parliament and ministers. Business is most adept at employing this channel. What local social forces require to be effective in federal fora is strong public support, a determined municipal government armed with some analytic expertise, and receptive provincial governments willing to amplify their voices. This works, at times, when business leads a broad local coalition that is united for the good of the whole community. Otherwise, local groups find it difficult to shift scale and operate at the federal level.

THE QUALITY OF POLICY

Our final area of analysis concerns the quality of the policies found in the field of federal property. How good are they? Are there ways that policy-making processes and policy outcomes could be improved? Some of the authors of the research presented here have addressed these questions only obliquely, but some evaluation needs to be made in the end. To do so, it is necessary to outline the criteria used to define good public policy. But first we must dismiss two criteria that can permeate discussions of policy-making in multilevel governance systems.

It is sometimes thought that having many governments involved in the policy process produces good public policy, or policy outputs that are superior to those produced by a single level of government acting alone. But there is no compelling reason to believe that complex intergovernmental relations mechanisms tend to produce better public policy. It is true that intergovernmental cooperation can bring more information to decision-making, and that it can overcome jurisdictional obstacles that stand in the way of coordinated and integrated policies. But this can come at a cost. When policy is produced by several governments acting in concert, it is hard for citizens to hold governments accountable for what they have done, because they can avoid individual responsibility. Further, the process of negotiation can consume much time and effort. The transaction costs mount as more governments become involved.

On the governance side, the debate is more complex. Some would argue that policy tends to be better when it is made and implemented in partnership with social forces (Leo 2006). This may seem a matter of equity and respect for citizens, but direct democracy does not lie at the core of the Canadian political system: ours is a representative democracy. Another argument for the participation of social forces is that individuals and groups can bring to the policy-making process expertise and information, especially about local conditions, that would otherwise not be available. This seems highly plausible, but it does not follow that local views should determine policy. Having input cannot necessarily be the same thing as making policy choices, because officials and elected politicians have other information and interests to take into account. This is quite obvious in the field of federal property, which is owned by the Crown in right of all Canadians. Many federal installations such as ports and parks are important to parties living far beyond the local community, and local communities are not well equipped to take those interests into account.

So if making decisions through multilevel governance is not necessarily associated with good public policy, what criteria can be used to evaluate policy? How do the policies about federal policy documented in the research collected here measure up against them? To begin, one straightforward criterion of the quality of policy is the speed with which it is formulated and implemented. Here the record is mixed. In Moncton, the CN Shop Yards were redeveloped expeditiously. With the province taking the lead, Chatham also moved quickly once the closure decision was finally made, and in Chilliwack many parties moved the adaptation forward without too much delay. Other cases proceeded very slowly. The Saint John Coast Guard site provides an example of snail-like progress. Perhaps harbour lands are particularly difficult to manage in a reasonable timeframe because of the multiple interests involved. In Toronto, the extraordinarily long process of dealing with waterfront lands was punctuated by another source of delay – the dramatic shifts over time in the personalities and ideologies bearing on redevelopment. In British Columbia, the claims on federal lands of First Nations produce delay. There continue to be disputes over the property used by the Port of Prince Rupert for its Fairview Container Terminal, not least because there are multiple First Nations' claims on the lands. Similar claims led to delays and controversy over the disposal of the Kapyong Barracks. In general, policy formulation in the federal property field is relatively slow.

Another criterion is policy coherence. Do the components of policies hang together in an integrated fashion or do they work at cross-purposes and leave gaps; further, are policies about individual cases congruent, or are there disparities across cases? It is clear from the research reported here that a standard, transparent, coherent federal land strategy is not in place in Canada. Our research shows there is a disjointed approach rather than a clear federal strategy, uniformly applied. This was most clearly seen in the case of the Saint John harbour, where two very different stewardship approaches were evident simultaneously. On the one hand, the Department of National Defence went to considerable effort to have its barracks building declared a municipal heritage site; on the other hand, Transport Canada seemed to have virtually abandoned its historic property on Partridge Island. The same lack of coherence can be seen in the federal government's handling of land divestiture. In some cases, the properties were sold to the Canada Lands Company, which in turn developed the lands for sale to others, as in Chilliwack and Moncton. In other instances, the land was virtually abandoned, with little federal involvement in mitigating the impacts on local communities, as in Argentia and Chatham. In some cases where the CLC has acquired surplus federal lands, the focus has been on maximizing the financial return from their development and sale. However, in other instances, facing strong political pressure to provide social benefits from redevelopment of the land, the CLC has turned properties over to separate subsidiary bodies, as at Downsview and the Old Port of Montreal, or divested its interest, as in the Kapyong barracks case in Winnipeg. So policy about federal lands is certainly not coherent overall.

Effectiveness is another criterion that is commonly used to judge the quality of public policy. Here, evaluation is difficult, because goals vary, and effectiveness is basically a measure of whether goals were attained. The cases of airport divestiture appear to have been effective. Airports are now functioning under local management, and Transport Canada has been relieved of the burden of subsidization (with costs essentially being transferred to the users). Cases involving the divestiture of surplus federal lands include some successes. The goal of finding viable alternative uses was largely met in Chilliwack, Downsview, and Moncton. Notably these were cases where the local economy was relatively diverse and vibrant, and where the federal activities, while significant, were not dominant. The process of disposing of land was much less successful in Chatham, Argentia, and Happy Valley–Goose Bay, which were close to being single-industry communities. The jury is still out on the Toronto waterfront. On that site, to date, effectiveness has been mixed at best, but there are many actors involved, and they have goals that are often in conflict.

Efficiency is yet another way to judge the quality of policy. Were goals achieved at a reasonable cost? This is difficult to evaluate when goals are unclear, for obvious reasons. It is also difficult because extensive accounting exercises are necessary to evaluate any case, and these are beyond the scope of the research undertaken here. Savoie (1995) provides a good example of such an analysis, focusing on the Summerside base closure in 1989. He first demonstrates the importance of the base to the community, in terms of payroll and military purchases. Then he compares Summerside's economic circumstances in 1986 and 1991. Most importantly, he calculates the savings from the base closure – an estimated $979 million over a fifteen-year period – and compares them with the one-time costs of helping the community to make the transition – about $63 million (1995, 69). Clearly the closure was efficient in strictly financial terms. It is likely that the other closures examined here were similarly efficient, from Ottawa's viewpoint, in cost-benefit terms.

But this discussion leads to a characteristic of federal property policy that is unique to the field. Policy-makers do consider effectiveness and efficiency when framing policy in any field, and they are also concerned about speed and policy coherence, just like the citizens and experts who evaluate the policy after the fact. But these considerations are outweighed by a simple fact about property: it has a value. Lands and installations have a market value, and this drives policy-making and the assessment of policy in a fundamental way. This issue speaks to another common criterion of good public policy – whether the problem is defined properly.

In other policy fields, of course, considerations of value are also involved, but they are rarely estimable with precision. What is the value, for example, of successfully integrating a new immigrant into the Canadian economy and society? Even if the person's economic contribution can be measured, no reasonable observer would agree that this is the whole story: that is, the only factor that should determine policy and provide the foundation for assessing how good it is. What is the value of spending money to improve the image of a municipality? We could measure the inflow of tourists and their spending patterns to help evaluate the policy. But again there are other considerations, such as the civic pride that image-building can bring to the local citizenry itself. In this manner, most policies in most fields are necessarily amorphous in their results, and debate about them is multifaceted.

Property is different. It has a value. This is whatever someone is willing to pay for it in a free-market transaction. And this consideration of price drives much policy about property. First, the value can be low or even zero. In such cases, there are few if any alternative uses for the property, as when the federal government seeks to abandon military bases in remote areas. As we have seen, this generates intense politics – the protests, the big coalitions, the working of every available political channel, the desperate delegations of businesspeople and municipal officials, and, ultimately, the plans for alternative uses, the demands for transitional assistance, and the pressure for long-term investment. The problem for policy-makers determined to close such facilities, when they are essentially worthless, is that any further spending is a subsidy, and this is perfectly transparent to all. Such expenditures can be very difficult to justify politically. So politicians, if they face enough pressure to induce them to subsidize, resort to investments. Ideally, these will have payoffs that are long-term and difficult to measure, such as the contributions at Chilliwack and the placement of offices to process the GST and gun registrations in Summerside and Miramichi. This kind of manoeuvre creates a lack of accountability. It can also lead to considerable inequity in how municipalities are treated, and, of course, equity is another criterion for assessing how good is policy.

The second effect of price occurs when the market value of property is relatively high. Then there is great pressure on policy-makers to realize the full property value. Maintaining a big expanse of parkland on a surplus site is difficult when the land could be used for condominiums or commercial development, and so could command a high price. Similarly, it is costly to insist on maintaining some proportion of low-rent housing in a complex where the market rents of apartments are expensive. Not to realize full market value implies that a subsidy is being provided. In cases such as this, similar to the low-value cases, the amount of the subsidy is perfectly evident. This can again cause political difficulties. The subsidy is a burden on taxpayers. But further, in the area of property, management and redevelopment are often carried out by semi-autonomous agencies, and these are generally set up with the requirement that they be self-financing. The Toronto Harbour Commission and Harbourfront provide two examples. The Canada Lands Company is another. This requirement creates a very strong incentive to maximize revenue, and this requires fully realizing the value of property, through either sales or redevelopment. Harbourfront, according to Sanderson and Filion, "promoted a rapid development of its land, favouring in the process financial gain over design principles and its affordable housing obligations." This pressure of the market continues on the Toronto waterfront. In late 2011, the influential councillor Doug Ford, who was pushing for rapid commercial development in the eastern waterfront, declared: "We need to develop the Port Lands. We need the revenue. We need to collect the $2 billion to $3 billion. It would be great for the city and our bottom line" (Church 2011). Similarly, a widely read columnist argued that the Port Lands were "the best chunk of real estate in the city, a prime development site ... Digging a new channel for the Don through the middle of it would squander that opportunity and wipe out a fortune in commercial value" (Gee 2011). Once the market value is clear, any policy that does not fully realize it involves a loss – a subsidy to something or someone.

The centrality of market prices makes federal property a unique policy field. The subsidies inherent in policies that deviate from the land's value make the field politically contestable. In instances where the market value is low, it is expedient to make investments whose payoff is less than fully transparent. Where land is valuable, the preservation of public amenity and social values can be done through strong planning frameworks and guidelines at the municipal level, in principle. But this is difficult when federal government departments and agencies resist. It is also technically difficult when the property is unique and the projects are large-scale. But there is a need for a better framework to handle the kinds of dynamic property issues explored in this volume; that is, for a system that is more predictable, equitable, transparent, and sensitive to local socio-economic conditions.

TOWARD A BETTER SYSTEM

We have found successes in some cases of dynamic federal-property issues. But this summary has also illuminated some common problems. Delay is one. Lack of coherence is another: policies are often ad hoc and uncoordinated in particular cases, and there is considerable disparity in the way property issues are managed across the country. Many instances of divestiture arouse fears and passions, leading to political turbulence and large losses to the community and to all actors involved, in the form of transaction costs. Most dynamic issues involve subsidies of various kinds, as market principles are bent by political pressure. Disparities in outcomes are apparent when the broad picture is surveyed. So equity – another feature of good public policy – is often not present in this field. There are also difficulties in the perennial issue areas, as municipal plans, zoning by-laws and regulations, and guidelines are bypassed and payments in lieu of taxes are determined unilaterally by federal authorities.

All of this indicates that the federal government needs to establish a more coordinated approach to its whole land management process. Federal installations and activities often become essential to local and regional economies. The sudden removal of these economic engines can be devastating to local communities. This is the most dramatic problem, but there are other reasons for the federal government to take a broader view of its stewardship of property and facilities. Essential public assets should not be considered solely from the market perspective embedded in the doctrines of New Public Management. Assets should not be seen simply as items that can provide a revenue source – as goods evaluated in light of current market conditions – but rather as public trusts to be managed carefully and disposed of judiciously. In instances of divestiture, the federal government should consider the effects carefully, and work with the local community to find appropriate alternative uses for those sites. Such care has marked some divestitures. In most instances of airport devolution, federal funding was extended to local airport authorities as part of the negotiation process to assist in the transition from federal to local operations. But this has not been true as a matter of policy in many other dynamic cases.

The lack of coordination and consistency in federal land dealings calls for the creation of a new agency – a Land Management Board – with appropriate authority to deal with all federal holdings. The Canada Lands Company could be one branch of this new Board. Others could deal with management and community interaction. The goal would be establishing a transparent, consistent, sensitive, and accountable process for the management and disposal of federal lands. The Board would have a perspective broader than the maximization of financial returns to one level of government. As the cliché has it, there is only one taxpayer. But all public lands can be regarded as belonging to all citizens and taxpayers rather than the specific level of government that is holding them. In this view, all levels of government along with local communities and their various social forces should have input into decisions about public lands.

Aspects of this need to consult have entered the mandate of the Canada Lands Company. The CLC's 2009–10 Annual Report is titled *Reaching Out*. It contains a modified mandate for the company – to "optimize the financial *and community* value of strategic properties that are no longer required for program purposes by the Government of Canada" (Canada Lands Company 2010, 1, emphasis added). As stated by the president and CEO, "2009–10 will stand out for the many opportunities it presented for CLC to reach out and collaborate effectively with various levels of government, the private sector, stakeholders and members of the public" (Canada Lands Company 2010, 2). But a new Land Management Board would take this orientation much further. It would be required to be cognizant and respectful of the land policies and regulations of the provinces and municipalities. This means that the municipality's plans and zoning and building by-laws would be adhered to by federal departments and agencies. PILTs would be fair and equitable and reflective of local taxation levels. The disposal of federal property would be discussed and negotiated with all stakeholders, as would compensation and assistance to replace the federal activities with suitable alternatives. The Land Management Board would be required to take adequate consideration of the social and economic implications of federal land disposal.

The CLC can take these implications into account, and it has done so in the past. But the CLC deals only with surplus properties. Federal departments vary widely in their approaches to public lands in their trust, and the new agency could harmonize this, by acting as an interface with other levels of government, especially municipal governments. It could also help coordinate departmental planning and consultation when more than one unit of the federal government is involved in a property or project.

All of this may seem reminiscent of efforts to take the politics out of policy. Such attempts are naive and quixotic. But the politics of dynamic property issues are unnecessarily painful and disruptive. Disposals provoke sharp reaction, and engender a highly politicized process that leads to inconsistent and inequitable results. The move toward a more transparent and accountable Land Management Board would imply a shift toward a more open regime that reflects the federal government's social license to operate within the community. This need to earn a social license from local communities is increasingly being recognized by the private sector and must be embraced by public agencies (Ircha 2012). Essentially a social license is a form of constructive engagement between federal landholders and their many stakeholders. Establishing a federal Land Management Board would be an essential first step in seeking a social license from local communities. As part of this, the Board could establish suitable appeal procedures to allow municipalities and social forces to question federal decisions about the management and disposal of property, compensation, and PILTs.

CONCLUSION

Federal property raises many important issues for municipal governments and citizens. Policies in this field constitute a fascinating area for study. Some issues are perennial, and are often perennial irritants because of federal high-handedness in areas such as PILTs and planning. The more visible issues are dynamic, generally involving the disposition of land and installations like airports, ports, and military bases. Since the federal presence generates local economic and social benefits, disposition represents a threat that is resisted strongly. The subsequent pattern is played out much the same in very different municipalities: there is concerted pressure, then an effort to engage the federal authorities in planning alternative uses for the property and making investments to cover the loss of economic activity. The results of this dynamic process are very uneven.

The federal government's approach to the management and disposition of its property tends to be disjointed and uncoordinated. There is also delay. Politics in this policy field are hard because lands have a market value that provides a ready measure of the subsidies that are being extended to achieve non-economic objectives. All of this suggests a need for an improved lands management and disposal process, one that involves not only maximizing the financial return from land and asset sales but also recognizing the broader social and economic issues that are significant for the local and regional community. To this end, a Land Management Board should be established to include the Canada Lands Company as one branch of an organization that has a broader mandate and that would ensure more consultation, transparency, equity, and accountability in the federal government's handling of public property.

NOTES

1 See Horak and Young (2012). The cities in which federal property was examined were Calgary, Charlottetown, Halifax, Montreal, Saskatoon, Toronto, and Winnipeg.
2 Reinforcing the municipal position toward the federal governments is one of several orientations that provincial governments can take toward municipal-federal relations: see Garcea and Pontikes (2006).
3 For the core source, see Osborne and Gaebler (1993); for a useful short account and a critique, see Denhart and Denhart (2000).
4 There are actually two entities. One is the Canada Lands Company Limited (CLCL), a non-agent federal Crown corporation; the other is its subsidiary company Canada Lands Company CLC Limited (CLC). For convenience, we refer simply to the CLC.

REFERENCES

Adam, M. 2010. "How Much Is This Building Worth? NCC and City at Loggerheads." *Ottawa Citizen*, 31 December.

Canada, Task Force on Program Review. 1986. *Real Property: A Study Team Report to the Task Force on Program Review*. Ottawa: Minister of Supply and Services Canada.

Canada Lands Company Limited. 1999. *Enhancing Communities Creating Value Annual Report 1998–1999*. n.p. Canada Lands Company Limited.

– 2010. *Reaching Out Annual Report 2009–2010*. n.p. Canada Lands Company Limited.

Church, Elizabeth. 2011. "Waterfront Toronto Open to Fast-Tracking Port Lands Makeover." *Globe and Mail*, 26 November.

Denhardt, Robert B., and Janet Vinzant Denhardt. 2000. "The New Public Service: Serving Rather than Steering." *Public Administration Review* 60, no. 6: 549–59.

Garcea, Joseph, and Ken Pontikes. 2006. "Federal-Municipal-Provincial Relations in Saskatchewan: Provincial Roles, Approaches, and Mechanisms." In *Canada: The State of the Federation 2004 – Municipal-Federal-Provincial Relations in Canada*, 333–67. Montreal & Kingston: McGill-Queen's University Press for the Institute of Intergovernmental Relations.

Gee, Marcus. 2011. "Don't Sink Waterfront Potential in Petty Local Politics." *Globe and Mail*, 31 December.

Goren, Lilly J., and P. Whitney Lackenbauer. 2003. "Closing Military Bases." In *The Government Taketh Away: The Politics of Pain in the United States and Canada*, edited by Leslie A. Pal and R. Kent Weaver, 167–93. Washington DC: Georgetown University Press.

Horak, Martin. 2012. "Multilevel Governance in Toronto: Success and Failure in Canada's Largest City." In *Sites of Governance: Multilevel Governance and Policy Making in Canada's Big Cities*, edited by Martin Horak and Robert Young, 228–62. Montreal & Kingston: McGill-Queen's University Press.

Horak, Martin, and Robert Young, eds. 2012. *Sites of Governance: Multilevel Governance and Policy Making in Canada's Big Cities*. Montreal & Kingston: McGill-Queen's University Press.

Ircha, Mike C. 2012. "Social License for Ports." *Canadian Sailings: Transportation and Trade Logistics*, 12 March: 17–22.

Osborne, David, and Ted Gaebler. 1993. *Reinventing Government: How the Entrepreneurial Spirit Is Transforming the Public Sector*. New York: Penguin.

Leo, Christopher. 2006. "Deep Federalism: Respecting Community Difference in National Policy." *Canadian Journal of Political Science* 39, no. 3: 481–506.

Lowi, Theodore J. 1964. "American Business, Public Policy, Case-Studies, and Political Theory." *World Politics* 16, no. 4: 677–715.

– 1972. "Four Systems of Policy, Politics, and Choice." *Public Administration Review* 32, no. 4: 298–310.

Savoie, Donald J. 1995. "Summerside: Revisiting the Base Closures." *Canadian Journal of Regional Science* 18, no. 1: 57–76.

Contributors

JEFF BRAUN-JACKSON is a former lecturer in political science at Memorial University of Newfoundland and is currently a researcher with the Ontario Professional Fire Fighters Association.

PIERRE FILION is a professor at the School of Planning of the University of Waterloo. His research interests include metropolitan scale planning, the implementation of smart growth strategies, and traditional and suburban downtowns.

MICHAEL C. IRCHA is a professor emeritus in civil engineering at the University of New Brunswick. His research encompasses municipal administration, urban planning, and ports planning, and he currently serves as senior advisor to the Association of Canadian Port Authorities.

LEONARD WADE LOCKE is a professor of economics at Memorial University of Newfoundland. He specializes in the Newfoundland and Labrador economy, resource economics, public finance, economic impact assessment, and cost-benefit analysis.

ROBERT MACKINNON is the vice-president of the University of New Brunswick in Saint John. His research interests include the historical geography of agriculture in Atlantic Canada, and urban and regional geography.

KURT PEACOCK is a historian and urban researcher, based in Saint John. In 2007–08, he was the Harold Crabtree Visiting Scholar in

New Brunswick Public Policy at UNB Saint John. He is the city columnist for the New Brunswick *Telegraph Journal.*

CHRISTOPHER SANDERSON is currently employed with the Government of Manitoba. His subjects of research interest include urban mega-projects, revitalization initiatives, and multi-stakeholder governance models.

TRACY SUMMERVILLE is an associate professor of political science at the University of Northern British Columbia. Her current research focuses on the impacts of globalization on northern BC.

STEPHEN TOMBLIN is a professor of political science and community health (medicine) at Memorial University of Newfoundland. He has written on regionalization, economic development, health restructuring, and human resource management and planning.

GARY N. WILSON is an associate professor of political science at the University of Northern British Columbia. His research focuses on politics and governance in the Arctic and in the Canadian provincial north.

JOHN YOUNG is the dean of the College of Arts, Social and Health Sciences at the University of Northern British Columbia and an associate professor of political science.

ROBERT YOUNG is a professor of political science at the University of Western Ontario, where he holds the Canada Research Chair in Multilevel Governance. He is the editor of the Fields of Governance series.